CONFEDERATE ORDEAL
The Southern Home Front

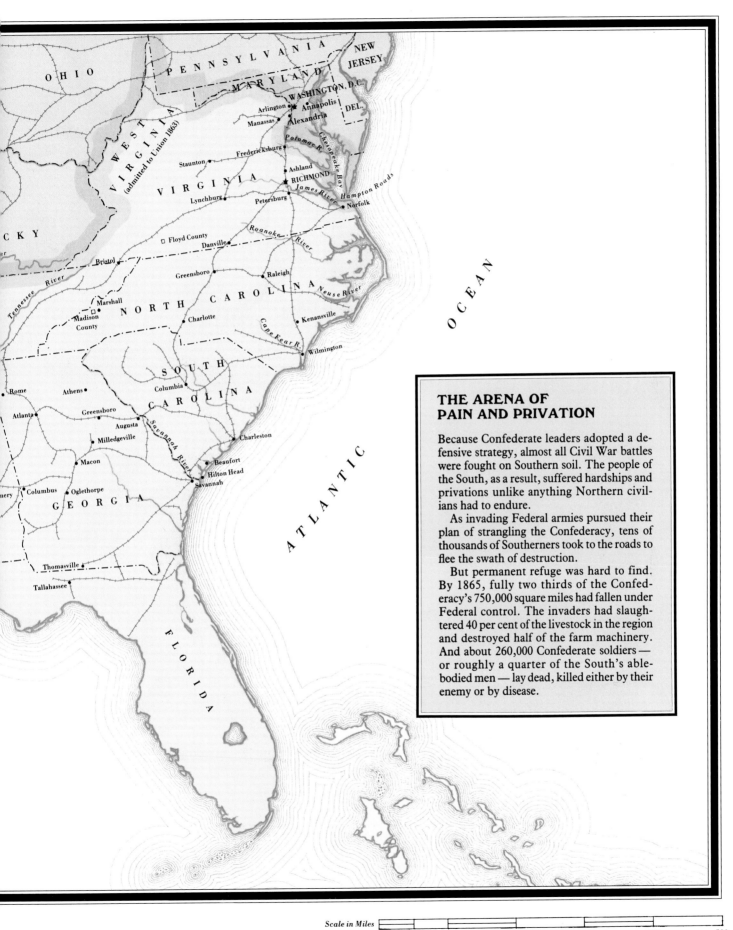

THE ARENA OF PAIN AND PRIVATION

Because Confederate leaders adopted a defensive strategy, almost all Civil War battles were fought on Southern soil. The people of the South, as a result, suffered hardships and privations unlike anything Northern civilians had to endure.

As invading Federal armies pursued their plan of strangling the Confederacy, tens of thousands of Southerners took to the roads to flee the swath of destruction.

But permanent refuge was hard to find. By 1865, fully two thirds of the Confederacy's 750,000 square miles had fallen under Federal control. The invaders had slaughtered 40 per cent of the livestock in the region and destroyed half of the farm machinery. And about 260,000 Confederate soldiers — or roughly a quarter of the South's able-bodied men — lay dead, killed either by their enemy or by disease.

Scale in Miles

0   50   100   200   300   400   500

TIME
LIFE
BOOKS

Other Publications:

AMERICAN COUNTRY
VOYAGE THROUGH THE UNIVERSE
THE THIRD REICH
THE TIME-LIFE GARDENER'S GUIDE
MYSTERIES OF THE UNKNOWN
TIME FRAME
FIX IT YOURSELF
FITNESS, HEALTH & NUTRITION
SUCCESSFUL PARENTING
HEALTHY HOME COOKING
UNDERSTANDING COMPUTERS
LIBRARY OF NATIONS
THE ENCHANTED WORLD
THE KODAK LIBRARY OF CREATIVE PHOTOGRAPHY
GREAT MEALS IN MINUTES
PLANET EARTH
COLLECTOR'S LIBRARY OF THE CIVIL WAR
THE EPIC OF FLIGHT
THE GOOD COOK
WORLD WAR II
HOME REPAIR AND IMPROVEMENT
THE OLD WEST

For information on and a full description of any of the
Time-Life Books series listed above, please call 1-800-621-
7026 or write:
Reader Information
Time-Life Customer Service
P.O. Box C-32068
Richmond, Virginia 23261-2068

This volume is one of a series that chronicles in full the
events of the American Civil War, 1861-1865.
Other books in the series include:

The Cover: A young Southern woman reads a letter
from a soldier in the family to a rapt audience of
relatives and slaves gathered around the porch. The
delivery of mail in the Confederacy was exceedingly
slow, and families often spent agonizing months
waiting to hear from their loved ones at the front.

THE
CIVIL
WAR

CONFEDERATE ORDEAL

BY

STEVEN A. CHANNING

AND THE

EDITORS OF TIME-LIFE BOOKS

The Southern Home Front

TIME-LIFE BOOKS, ALEXANDRIA, VIRGINIA

Time-Life Books Inc.
is a wholly owned subsidiary of

TIME INCORPORATED

FOUNDER: Henry R. Luce 1898-1967

Editor-in-Chief: Henry Anatole Grunwald
President: J. Richard Munro
Chairman of the Board: Ralph P. Davidson
Corporate Editor: Jason McManus
Group Vice President, Books: Reginald K. Brack Jr.
Vice President, Books: George Artandi

TIME-LIFE BOOKS INC.

EDITOR: George Constable
Executive Editor: George Daniels
Editorial General Manager: Neal Goff
Director of Design: Louis Klein
Editorial Board: Dale M. Brown, Roberta Conlan,
Ellen Phillips, Gerry Schremp, Donia Ann Steele,
Rosalind Stubenberg, Kit van Tulleken,
Henry Woodhead
Director of Research: Phyllis K. Wise
Director of Photography: John Conrad Weiser

PRESIDENT: William J. Henry
Senior Vice President: Christopher T. Linen
Vice Presidents: Stephen L. Bair, Edward Brash,
Robert A. Ellis, John M. Fahey Jr., Juanita T. James,
James L. Mercer, Wilhelm R. Saake, Paul R. Stewart,
Leopoldo Toralballa

The Civil War

Series Director: Henry Woodhead
Designer: Herbert H. Quarmby
Chief Researcher: Philip Brandt George

Editorial Staff for *Confederate Ordeal*
Associate Editors: R. W. Murphy, John Newton (text);
Loretta Britten, Jeremy Ross (pictures)
Text Editor: David Johnson
Staff Writers: William C. Banks, Allan Fallow,
Adrienne George, Glenn McNatt
Researchers: Harris J. Andrews (principal);
Susan V. Kelly, Brian C. Pohanka
Assistant Designer: Cynthia T. Richardson
Copy Coordinator: Stephen G. Hyslop
Picture Coordinator: Betty H. Weatherley
Editorial Assistant: Andrea E. Reynolds
Special Contributors: Ezra Bowen, Patricia Cassidy-
Lewis, Jane S. Hanna, Margaret Johnson Sliker

Editorial Operations
Design: Ellen Robling (assistant director)
Copy Chief: Diane Ullius
Editorial Operations: Caroline A. Boubin (manager)
Production: Celia Beattie
Quality Control: James J. Cox (director)
Library: Louise D. Forstall

Correspondents: Elisabeth Kraemer-Singh (Bonn);
Margot Hapgood, Dorothy Bacon (London); Miriam
Hsia (New York); Maria Vincenza Aloisi, Josephine
du Brusle (Paris); Ann Natanson (Rome). Valuable
assistance was also provided by: Carolyn Chubet
(New York).

Library of Congress Cataloguing in Publication Data
Channing, Steven A.
    Confederate ordeal.
    (The Civil War)
    Bibliography: p.
    Includes index.
    1. Confederate States of America — History. I. Time-
Life Books.   II. Title.   III. Series.
E487.C48 1984   973.7'13   83-17988
ISBN 0-8094-4728-2
ISBN 0-8094-4729-0 (lib. bdg.)

The Author:
Steven A. Channing is the author of the Allen Nevins
Award-winning study *Crisis of Fear: Secession in South
Carolina* and of *Kentucky,* a volume in the Bicentennial
States and the Nation history series. Working in film and
video, he has produced three documentaries: *This Other
Eden, Upon This Rock* and *The N.C. 400 Minutes,* which
celebrates North Carolina's 400th anniversary.

The Consultants:
Colonel John R. Elting, USA (Ret.), a former Associate
Professor at West Point, is the author of *Battles for Scandi-
navia* in the Time-Life Books World War II series and of
*The Battle of Bunker's Hill, The Battles of Saratoga, Mili-
tary History and Atlas of the Napoleonic Wars* and *American
Army Life.* He is also editor of the three volumes of *Military Uniforms in America, 1755-1867,* and associate editor
of *The West Point Atlas of American Wars.*

James I. Robertson Jr. is C. P. Miles Professor of History
at Virginia Tech. The recipient of the Nevins-Freeman
Award and other prizes in the field of Civil War history, he
has written or edited some 20 books, which include *The
Stonewall Brigade, Civil War Books: A Critical Bibliogra-
phy* and *Civil War Sites in Virginia.*

William A. Frassanito, a Civil War historian and lecturer
specializing in photograph analysis, is the author of two
award-winning studies, *Gettysburg: A Journey in Time* and
*Antietam: The Photographic Legacy of America's Bloodiest
Day,* and a companion volume, *Grant and Lee, The Virginia Campaigns.* He has also served as chief consultant to the
photographic history series *The Image of War.*

Les Jensen, Curator of the U.S. Army Transportation
Museum at Fort Eustis, Virginia, specializes in Civil War
artifacts and is a conservator of historic flags. He is a
contributor to *The Image of War* series, consultant for
numerous Civil War publications and museums, and a
member of the Company of Military Historians. He was
formerly Curator of the Museum of the Confederacy in
Richmond, Virginia.

Michael McAfee specializes in military uniforms and has
been Curator of Uniforms and History at the West Point
Museum since 1970. A fellow of the Company of Military
Historians, he coedited with Colonel Elting *Long Endure:
The Civil War Years,* and he collaborated with Frederick
Todd on *American Military Equipage.* He has written nu-
merous articles for *Military Images Magazine,* as well as
Artillery of the American Revolution, 1775-1783.

Charles East is Assistant Director and Editor at the University of Georgia Press in Athens, and author of *The Face
of Louisiana* and *Baton Rouge: A Civil War Album.* Specializing in 19th Century photographs of the South, he has
contributed to numerous publications on the Civil War,
including *The Image of War* series.

CONTENTS

The Pulse of Independence

"We are without machinery, without means, and threatened by a powerful opposition; but I do not despond, and will not shrink from the task imposed on me."

JEFFERSON DAVIS

1

Sometime after he enlisted in the Confederate Army in 1861, the young Georgia poet Sidney Lanier attended a mock medieval tournament in Kinston, North Carolina. He came away enraptured. In the spectacle of mounted Confederate officers dressed as knights competing for the honor of a local belle, he saw a metaphor for the entire Civil War. The South was a gallant knight tilting against the darkly materialistic forces of the North in defense of a hallowed ideal of chivalry. The Confederacy's war, wrote Lanier, had "the sanctity of a religious cause" arrayed in "military trappings."

In fact, gallantry was a main strength of the Confederacy — the almost irrepressible force that sustained the South for four years against overwhelming odds. Yet Lanier's view was misleading. The romantic tournament and the men who staged it represented only the narrow elite of Southern society. The wealthy planters who led the South into the War — and indeed perceived of themselves as ennobled in person and chivalric in nature — constituted only one half of one per cent of a total population of nine million. Moreover, theirs was an aristocracy of property, not of birth. Most of them were self-made men from ordinary backgrounds whose influence and status was measured in the number of slaves they owned and the acreage of their plantations. The planters had the leisure and wealth to pursue politics; thus they formed the leadership of the Confederacy.

Only about one fourth of white families in 1860 owned any slaves at all, and 50 per cent of this group owned no more than five. Well over half the Southern people made up a middle class of farmers who tilled no more than 100 acres, land they generally worked themselves or with a few slaves or hired hands. The farmers cared little for a chivalric ideal and were often at odds with the planters in state and local politics. They did, however, share the economic goals of their planter neighbors; in many cases they hoped to acquire plantations themselves. Like all Southerners, they tended to be clannish and sturdily independent — so much so that many of them would resist the impositions of the Confederate government.

At the bottom of the economic ladder were the South's two million or so impoverished whites — called "peckerwoods" or "poor whites" — who survived by hunting and fishing in the mountains or pine barrens, where the soil was poor.

But though the people of this intensely rural society differed dramatically in their circumstances and perceptions, most remained conservative in their traditions. Southerners of all classes and locales were fervently committed to the idea of an agrarian life that had shaped their economy and culture for two centuries. Rich or poor, they valued the land, not only for the sustenance or profit it provided, but also because it bred, as an editor wrote, "an inherent dignity and independence" in those who lived by it. Moreover,

President Jefferson Davis was both revered and scorned by Southerners, but never fully understood. An associate called him "the Sphinx of the Confederacy."

Southerners felt that an agrarian society produced individuals of higher moral character than that exhibited by the people of the urban North—who were said in the Southern press to exalt "the steam engine and the electric telegraph above God." A major fear of tradition-bound Southerners was that in struggling to be born, the Confederacy would turn itself into a replica of the vulgar Northern mercantile society from which it was trying to break.

Ingrained in Southern conservatism was an irony that haunted the Confederacy from its founding. Here was a nation created to defend the status quo—yet compelled from the outset by war to generate enormous economic and social change. The dual burden of such upheaval and military invasion put tremendous strains on a society that had resisted change for generations. Planters found their traditional sources of wealth cut off, and a fledgling mercantile class rose to prominence. Women formed a new working class in the war industries and assumed the management of plantations and farms in the absence of their men. Hardships hit rich and poor alike, and many people found themselves working at jobs for which nothing in their backgrounds had prepared them.

Money in this strange society became virtually worthless, and rail travel almost impossible. People by the tens of thousands took to the roads to flee the invading armies. The cities swelled with refugees and grew desperately short of food. Although haunted by nightmares of black insurrection, the South was compelled to turn over the burden of slave management to women, children and old men.

In the South as in the North, loyalty to state and locale were stronger than a sense of national duty, and under the relentless pressure of war, internal dissent sharpened dramatically in many parts of the South. Even rock-ribbed Confederates grew increasingly hostile toward a government that seemed powerless to ease their misery and reverse the fading fortunes of the Confederacy. The populace chafed at a succession of harsh wartime measures, including income-tax, conscription and impressment laws. As defeat loomed, military desertions grew epidemic, and violence broke out in pockets of the home front.

The changes wrought on the southland in the course of the conflict were so numerous and profound that a Louisiana woman could write that she was living not only out of place but "out of time," in some curious limbo with no past or future.

Yet the wonder is that the people of the Confederacy carried on. Threatened with imminent destruction, they responded for the most part with great courage, resilience and even humor. In some, the crisis of the Confederacy even generated a kind of exhilaration—a sense that out of the travail a new nation was evolving.

The birth of the Confederacy was far more painful than sublime. Not surprisingly, the hastily created government reflected many of the doubts and hesitations that would agitate the bulk of the population. Like the U.S. government, the Confederate government was theoretically divided into three equal branches—executive, legislative and judicial. Actually, the Confederacy never had a Supreme Court because Congressmen could never agree on the extent of its authority over the high courts of the individual states. The Congress, furthermore, became subordinate to the executive branch under the pressure of war.

The 28 Senators and 122 Representatives of the Confederate First Congress were mostly of the wealthy professional or planter class to whom Southerners looked for leadership. A third of the officials elected during the War had served in the United States Congress, and some were still sympathetic to the idea of union and hoped for an acceptable reconciliation. Others had been in the legislatures of their various states and were not readily inclined to allow the Confederacy's national priorities to intrude on their home loyalties. Nonetheless, the public expected great things of them — for Southerners by and large believed that a slave-based society produced superior statesmen on the model of George Washington, Thomas Jefferson or James Madison.

At first most of the men in government, anxious to live up to this image of statesmanship, promoted unity in support of the war effort. But many Congressmen soon found themselves in the uncomfortable position of Senator Herschel V. Johnson of Georgia, who "acquiesced in what I could not approve" merely to avoid appearing divisive.

The uneasy truce evaporated as the passion for independence that had driven the South out of the Union erupted into dissension. Lacking a system of political parties that might have organized bloc support for or against a piece of legislation, the Congress sank into confusion as each legislator voted his whim on every issue. "You would be amazed," wrote Georgia Congressman Warren Akin to his wife, "to see the differences of opinion that exist among the members. It seems, sometimes, that no proposition, however plain and simple, could be made that would not meet with opposition."

Those opposed to the policies of Jefferson Davis berated the President and his supporters, while Congressmen of all persuasions joined in flaying the President's Cabinet. Calmer voices urged restraint: "The crew may not like their captain, but if they are mad enough to mutiny while a storm is raging, all hands are bound to go to the bottom," observed Senator William Lowndes Yancey of Alabama. But in the charged atmosphere of Richmond, such warnings were infrequently heeded.

Even without this kind of internecine warfare, the Congress was working under severe handicaps. Many of the South's ablest leaders, convinced that the place of honor was in the field, had deserted politics to enter the Army. Others left for the military after serving in Congress only a few months.

Absenteeism was another problem. Members who represented so-called imaginary constituencies — districts swallowed by the Federal armies — often felt little obligation to appear in Congress regularly, and they were bitterly resented by more conscientious Representatives.

There was so much truancy, in fact, that important business sometimes had to be delayed for lack of a quorum. Rumors circulated of rampant drunkenness among the legislators. South Carolinian James H. Hammond wrote to Confederate Senator Robert M. T. Hunter: "Some malign influence seems to preside over your councils. Pardon me, is the majority always drunk?"

The Confederate Congress suffered, too, from lack of strong direction at the top. As Vice President, Alexander Hamilton Stephens of Georgia was President of the Senate, but he rarely appeared there after 1862.

12

Frail and suffering from neuralgia and rheumatism, he insisted that he was too weak to make the journey from his Georgia home to Richmond. His real reason was that he had lost faith in the Confederacy, and particularly in Jefferson Davis — whose policies, he was convinced, were leading to military dictatorship. Stephens snidely professed "no more feeling of resentment" toward Davis than he had "toward the defects and infirmities of my poor old blind and deaf dog." The Vice President's attitude undoubtedly influenced opinion in the Congress, adding to Davis' difficulties there.

The Davis supporters in Congress were basically the men who accepted the necessity of a strong central authority and some temporary sacrifice of civil liberties to win the War. The most passionate anti-Davis men were the states' righters, who fought every move toward centralization as a step toward tyranny. The persistent conflict between these two forces added to the weakness of the Congress, which seemed to become more rowdy as it became more ineffectual.

A celebrated free-for-all occurred during one of the futile attempts to establish the Confederate Supreme Court. Opponents feared that President Davis would pack the Court with his favorites — notably the much-disliked Secretary of War, Judah P. Benjamin — and use it to enhance the power of the executive. When Senator Benjamin H. Hill, chairman of the Judiciary Committee, introduced a bill for the creation of the Court, he was violently opposed by Alabama Senator Yancey, who accused Hill of some flagrant misrepresentations. Hill promptly hurled an inkstand at Yancey, cutting his cheek, and then rushed at him with a chair before colleagues quelled the combat.

On a few other occasions, fist fights broke out in Congress, providing what Alexander Stephens called from his haven in Georgia "some of the most disgraceful scenes ever enacted by a legislative body." When Congress met in secret session, ostensibly to discourage excessive oratory, the Richmond *Examiner* suggested that the members had "locked themselves away from the newspapers that they might drink whisky excluded from the observations of the world." Critics depicted the legislators as "weak, sycophantic and trifling," and accused them of cowardice when they hastily adjourned at the first threat to Richmond by General George B. McClellan's army in early May 1862; the Richmond *Whig* satirized the legislators as fleeing in a canalboat drawn by docile mules and protected by ladies armed with popguns. If these "enemies of Liberty" refused to resign, raged the Athens, Georgia, *Southern Watchman*, they should be "hung like dogs."

Yet the Congress, for all its faults, was not as consistently dilatory and trifling as its detractors claimed. In the course of its stormy sessions, it did establish a new government and bureaucracy. It managed to organize the first national military draft on the North American continent, passed enabling laws to develop war industries and set up a graduated income tax.

The men appointed to Jefferson Davis' Cabinet were also uneven in their abilities and achievements. The President filled the six Cabinet positions mostly on the basis of political considerations, with each appointee coming from a different state. All of the Cabinet members were slaveowners and most were self-made men who had risen to places of prominence in their respective states. Treasury Secretary Christopher G.

Memminger was a German immigrant, Postmaster General John H. Reagan the son of a tanner, Attorney General Judah P. Benjamin the son of a small merchant, and Secretary of the Navy Stephen R. Mallory the son of a widowed boarding-house keeper. Only Secretary of State Robert Toombs and Secretary of War Leroy Walker were born to wealth.

The turnover in the more sensitive positions — Davis had four secretaries of state, five attorneys general, six secretaries of war — resulted in part from increasing attacks by factions in Congress that thought the Cabinet members were mere mouthpieces for Davis. The President's opposition, according to a Richmond newspaper, viewed his Cabinet as a "set of old fogy broken down politicians, who act as mere clerks to the President."

In fact, the President encouraged Cabinet members to speak their minds. But while most of them were reasonably competent men, they were not perceptive enough to cope with the critical problems of the War. There were notable exceptions. James A. Seddon of Virginia, a successful planter and

President Jefferson Davis (*fourth from left*) and his Cabinet flank General Robert E. Lee as he explains strategy on a map inside their council chamber at Richmond. The Northern artist who created this scene took an ironic shortcut: Working from an illustration of Lincoln and his Cabinet, he merely affixed the faces of the Confederates onto the bodies of their Federal counterparts.

an ardent secessionist, brought energy and imagination to the office of Secretary of War. Seddon recognized the weakness of the government's fragmented military strategy in the West and moved to establish a unified command in that theater. He also attempted to extend central control over the South's chaotic transportation system and encouraged intensified efforts to import much-needed supplies by running the Federal blockade. Seddon lasted longer in office than any other secretary of war, and when he was finally pressured to resign in February of 1865, it was more a reflection of Congress' frustration with military reversals than a judgment on his conduct of office.

Another outstanding Cabinet member was Judah Benjamin, sometimes said to be "the most brilliant man in the Confederate government." Born in the West Indies of Jewish parents, Benjamin had been a successful lawyer and sugar planter in New Orleans before winning election to the Louisiana state legislature and later to the United States Senate. As Davis' attorney general, he organized the new Confederate Department of Justice and became the Cabinet officer on whom the President chiefly relied. Later he reorganized the War and State Departments while serving as the head of each.

Blamed for military setbacks in Tennessee at Forts Henry and Donelson while he was at the War Department, Benjamin came under increasing attack, made more violent by anti-Semitism and jealousy of his closeness to the President. "A grander rascal than this Jew Benjamin does not exist in the Confederacy," declared the fiery Confederate Congressman from Georgia, Thomas R. R. Cobb. Others spoke of "Christianizing" the Cabinet by removing Benjamin, claiming that he had influenced the President to omit the name of Christ from his proclamations for public prayers.

The tensions and animosities that plagued Confederate public life owed something to the character of Jefferson Davis himself. As a U.S. Senator from Mississippi before the War, he had been heard to declare in floor debate, "I make no terms; I accept no compromises." That inflexibility, backed by a conviction of righteousness, made it difficult at times for even his admirers to warm to him. His critics took his stubbornness for arrogance, and his determination for unreasoning ambition. Some of his bitterest enemies in the Congress called him "Majesty Davis," and compared him with the hated Abraham Lincoln. Davis' rigidity often involved him in quarrels, and as a journalist who knew him remarked, he was as "unforgiving as a Spaniard to those whom he fancies his foes."

The President's temper and his personal relations were undoubtedly made more difficult by poor health. Described by his wife as "a nervous dyspeptic by habit," he was also blind in one eye and afflicted by partial facial paralysis.

Davis steadfastly refused to court popular favor, and sometimes seemed to go out of his way to alienate associates. In a typically blunt note, he reprimanded Confederate General Pierre G. T. Beauregard for trying "to exalt yourself at my expense" in a military report on the first battle of Manassas. To an acquaintance who wrote the President in hopes of obtaining a commission, Davis replied brusquely that no "recital of service rendered" would ever influence his appointments.

There were other sides to the Davis character — a sense of compassion, for example, that led him to commute every death sentence for desertion that came across his desk, with the explanation that "the poorest use" of a soldier was "to shoot him." It was the same compassion that prompted him to scrawl replies to thousands of Southerners in distress. The public rarely saw this side of the President, and the bureaucrats around him deplored it as a distraction from more important responsibilities. Davis, for example, once took the time to reply to a widow's complaint that the Confederate cavalry had stolen her hogs.

War Department clerk John Beauchamp Jones recalled how Davis came to his office looking for a piece of mail. When Jones told him it was buried somewhere in a "half a bushel" of letters waiting to be filed, the President without hesitation began burrowing into the pile. "We removed them one by one," wrote Jones, "and as we progressed, he said with an impatient smile, 'It is always sure to be the last one.' And so it was."

Richmond lawyer George W. Randolph, who served for a time as secretary of war, was less tolerant. Although he was fond of Davis, he found him a deplorable executive. Davis lacked any kind of "system," wrote Randolph; he was "very slow," and above all, had no capacity to discriminate between the "important and unimportant."

Yet despite the criticism and vituperations, Davis somehow gave the Confederacy a sense of identity and purpose. His "energy, sagacity, and indomitable will," wrote a *New York Times* reporter who met him, was all that kept the Confederacy going. He might be "cold, reserved, imperious," but "he could be the tool of no man; without him, the Rebellion would crumble to pieces in a day."

James Dunwoody Brownson De Bow, the Charleston-born editor of *De Bow's Review*, urged the South to develop its industry in order to "beat the Yankees with their own tools."

That estimate may have been exaggerated, but certainly many Southerners saw in Davis' tall, erect figure the visual embodiment of their hopes for a Southern nation that could stand alone.

No group was more hopeful about the future of the Confederacy than a small coterie of industrial promoters who for a decade had been preaching that the salvation of the South lay in the development of industry. During the expansive years of the 1850s, many Southern cities had experienced a considerable growth in commerce, banking and manufacture. Indeed, Southern industrialization amounted to a quiet — and, to many planters, an insidious — internal revolution.

By the start of the War the region had developed a small skilled-labor force made up of native whites, slaves and free blacks, and Irish and German immigrants. Equally important, it had a pool of managers able to make good use of this labor force, and gradually to expand it.

The new industrial movement even had a spokesman. He was New Orleans journalist James D. B. De Bow, who published the highly influential *De Bow's Review*. In editorial after editorial, De Bow argued that if the South did not continue to industrialize, it would find itself increasingly in bondage to Northern industry.

De Bow and other industrial promoters believed that the War and Lincoln's attempted blockade were not evils but blessings. Just as the War of 1812 and the British blockade had accelerated the rise of industry in New England, so would the War Between the States now aid the South.

When the struggle was barely six months old, De Bow journeyed north to Richmond to inspect a group of massive brick buildings clustered below Gamble's Hill on the banks of the James River. This noisy caldron of activity was the home of the Tredegar Iron Works. With Tredegar's owner and manager, Joseph Reid Anderson, as his guide, De Bow walked through the cavernous foundry. His excitement mounted at every step. Here were huge cannon, great rifled naval guns, shells and railroad iron. Through a haze of smoke from the forges moved nearly 1,500 skilled workers. "The capacity of the establishment is almost without limit," De Bow reported. "It seems like a special providence that it exists." He added that his fears for the Confederate nation had been eased: The Confederacy had it in its power to become a great workshop.

Thanks to the War, De Bow exulted, "every branch of manufacturing is springing up." This movement fed a burgeoning sense of regional pride. A Mississippi journalist recalled that before the War, "we were so poor, and so helpless, the Yankees had to take care of us like so many children. Let us resolve never more to be dependent on that people who are murdering us." The Charles-ton *Mercury* reported hearing daily of "new schemes and designs — manufactures, arts, sciences. We shall soon be able to produce every cannon and gun, every pistol and sabre, every rifle and spear."

The man who presided over the Confederate armaments program was an enormously resourceful transplanted Yankee named Josiah Gorgas. A former officer in the United States Ordnance Department, Gorgas became Chief of Confederate Ordnance in 1861 and quickly made his bureau one of the few great successes of the Confederate government.

When he took over, Gorgas found that the Confederacy had about 160,000 small arms seized from Federal arsenals within the several states. That was scarcely enough. Casting about for other sources, he discovered that Northern munitions manufacturers had few scruples about selling. On the day of Lincoln's inauguration, Colonel Samuel Colt, head of the Colt's Patent Fire Arms Company of Hartford, Connecticut, had shrewdly sent a brace of pistols as a gift to Howell Cobb of Georgia, President of the provisional Confederate Congress. Taking the hint, Gorgas dispatched arms buyers to the North and established a limited traffic in handguns that continued through neutral Kentucky even after the fall of Fort Sumter and the first battle at Manassas.

In addition, Gorgas sent arms buyers to Europe and bought four blockade runners to ferry their purchases through the net of Federal warships. And he urged the troops to recover Federal arms and ammunition from the battlefield; early in the War cartridges and shells were in such short supply, noted a Confederate officer, that "in every battle we fight we must capture as much am-

A blockade runner reaches the Confederate shore after eluding Federal warships.

Vital Cargoes from Abroad

"An iron steamer has run the blockade at Savannah," a South Carolina woman wrote in September 1861. "We raise our wilted heads like flowers after a shower." Her joy was understandable; the South depended on blockade runners for vital war matériel.

Josiah Gorgas, head of the Confederate Ordnance Bureau, described in his journal the indispensable role of these small, swift ships. "Our freight steamers continue to run to Bermuda," he wrote on August 2, 1863. "This is our chief source of supply for arms; and we get our steel, tin, zinc in this way. We also import leather, tools, hardware, medicines, saltpeter, lead in large quantities."

All told, the blockade runners provided the South with about 600,000 stand of arms, most of them British-made Enfield rifles.

Smuggled through the blockade from England during the final months of the War, this camp chest was used by Jefferson Davis during his flight after the fall of Richmond in April 1865.

A sampling of items brought to the South through the blockade includes a five-shot revolver, a woman's hat, a woolen army jacket, a lead ingot needed for manufacturing bullets, field glasses and a kit of surgical instruments. The bonnet was frivolous, of course, but a ready market existed for such morale-boosting luxury items.

.44-CALIBER BRITISH KERR REVOLVER

STRAW BONNET

CONFEDERATE ARMY JACKET

LEAD INGOT

FIELD GLASSES

SURGICAL KIT

munition as we use." The men managed to do so during the largely successful Eastern campaigns of 1861 and 1862 — capturing 100,000 stand of enemy arms in 1862 alone. The Macon *Daily Telegraph* went so far as to print a jingle urging the grim practice: "Want a weapon? Why, capture one! / Every Doodle has got a gun, / Belt and bayonet, bright and new; / Kill a Doodle, and capture two!"

But these were at best uncertain sources of supply, intended only to tide the Confederacy over until its own arms industry could provide all that was needed. A survey of existing resources told Gorgas that the South had virtually all the materials it required for building up its war capacity. Iron and coal were plentiful. There were scattered deposits of most other munitions ingredients except mercury, for percussion caps; and mercury could be shipped through Texas from Mexico.

Under Gorgas' direction, the Confederacy began establishing its own arsenals, cannon foundries, powder mills, forges, smelting works, rolling mills, and carbine and pistol factories. It underwrote new, privately owned facilities by lending manufacturers start-up funds in exchange for their pledge to sell most or all of the plants' production to the military. And the government encouraged the expansion of existing plants by granting their owners substantial contracts. Despite the South's traditional distrust of bureaucratic interference, the Confederate government monitored production and even put a ceiling on profits.

One of the Ordnance Bureau's most spectacular achievements was in the manufacture of gunpowder, a process requiring supplies of charcoal, sulfur and niter, or saltpeter.

The Confederate States had plenty of sulfur and charcoal but lacked adequate supplies of niter.

A group of ordnance officers known as the Niter Corps canvassed the South and finally found substantial niter deposits in the limestone caves of eastern Tennessee and northern Alabama.

To supplement this natural supply, the bureau resorted to a European method of production involving so-called nitriaries. Shallow pits were dug and filled with organic matter: animal carcasses, manure and vegetable scraps. Stagnant water was then poured over the lot, along with urine collected from nearby communities. After decomposing for 18 months, this noisome compost was shoveled into hoppers and thoroughly leached with water—from which the niter was finally removed.

The Ordnance Bureau next turned its attention to the construction of gunpowder manufacturing facilities, the largest of which was to be in Augusta, Georgia. Construction on such an ambitious scale proved extremely difficult in the wartime South, which lacked the tool-making facilities to create heavy machinery. Again ordnance

Richmond's Tredegar Iron Works, a foundry owned and managed by General Joseph Reid Anderson, cast 1,099 cannon during the War — near half of all the artillery pieces manufactured in the Confederacy.

The Augusta, Georgia, powder works, designed and built by Colonel George Washington Rains, opened in April of 1862 and was soon producing as much as ,000 pounds of gunpowder a day.

officers searched the South for essentials.

When the Augusta powder mill began operations in 1862 it was a patchwork of components from virtually the entire Confederacy. Five-ton iron rollers came from Richmond; an immense cast-iron shaft from Chattanooga; a fine, 130-horsepower steam engine from Atlanta; iron castings from Alabama; steampipes from New Orleans; copper boilers cannibalized from turpentine stills at Wilmington, North Carolina. Yet this jerrybuilt facility turned out to be one of the most productive powder mills on the continent. In the three remaining years of the War it produced 2,750,000 pounds of high-quality gunpowder.

The grandest triumph of all Confederate war industries, however, continued to be Richmond's Tredegar Iron Works, which came to be known as the mother arsenal of the new nation. Tredegar's director, Joseph Anderson, pledged all-out service to his government early in the War in a succinct telegram: "Will make anything you want — work night and day if necessary, and ship by rail." He was as good as his word. The Richmond plant turned out more than a thousand cannon, including many large siege guns;

enormous quantities of artillery projectiles; naval mines; gun carriages; experimental submersible vessels; armor plating and machinery for warships; and much heavy equipment for other arsenals springing up about the South.

As a center of research, the firm conceived and developed new armaments, including the superior Brooke rifled naval gun. In time, Tredegar became so complex an operation that Anderson bought coal mines and blast furnaces to assure his own crude-metal supply, and clothed his 2,500 workers by building his own tannery and shoe factory and running cloth through the blockade from Bermuda in his own boats. So crucial did the Richmond works become to the Confederate war effort that General Robert E. Lee urged Davis to disperse some of the company's munitions production across the Confederacy, so that if the capital should fall, "we would not be destitute."

The fear of losing important manufacturing centers to the advancing Union armies haunted the Confederacy's industrial planners throughout the War. When Nashville fell to the Union in 1862, the Confederacy lost two powder mills and important ordnance stores established there by Josiah Gorgas. The loss of New Orleans that same year deprived the Confederacy of its most important manufacturing city after Richmond. With the fall of Vicksburg in 1863 and the subsequent Federal blockade of the Mississippi, the mercury supply from Mexico was virtually cut off and the manufacture of percussion caps seriously impeded. Braxton Bragg's defeat at Chattanooga at the end of 1863 cut off the Tennessee copper mines and left the Confederates so short of copper that they had to stop making their favorite ar-

Headquarters
53d Reg't N. C. Militia,
Fayetteville, April 18, 1862.
I am authorized by the Adjutant General of the State to purchase
DOUBLE-BARREL SHOT-GUNS and GOOD RIFLES,
for the use of the Militia of Cumberland county. Any persons having Guns of the proper description can get the full value in *Cash*, by passing them in to A. M. Johnson, Quartermaster, or Dr. Theo. Martine, Ordnance Officer of the Regiment. All Officers are requested to disseminate this information and to facilitate the purchase of Arms for the purpose named.
JOHN H. COOK,
Col. Com'dg.

A broadside seeking weapons for North Carolina's state militia offers to pay "the full value in *Cash*" for desperately needed shotguns and rifles. Before rampant inflation made cash nearly worthless, most citizens responded readily to these appeals.

tillery piece, the bronze Napoleon cannon.

Fortunately for the Confederacy, the Tredegar Iron Works continued to turn out armaments until Richmond itself fell in the last days of the War. But in the meantime Tredegar and other war factories were threatened by another problem that plagued every Southern manufacturer — where to get the personnel to man the production lines? The problem became critical in the spring of 1862, when the Confederate Congress passed a conscription act establishing a military draft.

In theory, all workers engaged in war industries were exempt; in practice, local draft boards anxious to fill their quotas often drafted industrial workers in violation of the law. Moreover, some individual states permitted men exempted from the national service to be placed on active duty in the state militia. In one such case, the Richmond Armory reported that its production fell off by at least 360 rifles per month after an expert barrel straightener was called to serve in the militia and later killed in the defense of Richmond.

Perhaps most serious of all, the Confederate conscription laws did not clearly state the status of foreign-born workers, many of whom were trained artisans. A large proportion of officers' swords, for example, were turned out either by Austrian artisans working in a small firm in Kenansville, North Carolina, or by German workers in the firm of Louis Haiman and Brother in Columbus, Georgia. Workers trained in England and Germany played an essential role at the Tredegar Iron Works. Many of these men fled to the North or back to their own countries when they learned that they were about to be drafted.

The Confederate War Department, recognizing the problem, wrote rules exempting foreigners who declared themselves temporary residents. But the amendment was subject to the approval of local draft boards, and many of them ignored it. By the summer of 1863, Tredegar had lost so many skilled puddlers, whose job was handling molten iron, that only a third of the furnaces in the rolling mill were functioning.

One obvious way to relieve the labor shortage was by using some of the 3.5 million slaves toiling on Southern plantations. A few of these had already been impressed by the military to work on fortifications. In 1863 Congress authorized widespread impressment of slaves, along with compensation for their masters. These blacks served as teamsters, cooks, hospital attendants, construction workers, and as skilled or unskilled laborers in many industrial plants.

But there was strong resistance to a wider use of slave labor. Planters feared that their valuable property would be abused by careless managers. Slaves were often held by the government longer than promised, and the government was slow to pay its bills.

Much of the opposition to such impressment, however, stemmed from a fear that any experience away from the plantation was likely to give the slaves a dangerous taste for independence. A slave infected with "strange philosophies," wrote South Carolina Senator James Hammond, might easily come home and "demoralize a dozen negro settlements."

Finding that further appeals for slave labor produced little response, the government and some states passed additional legislation in 1863 that provided owners higher rates of compensation for requisitioned slaves. While Confederate soldiers were receiving $11 a month, for example, Alabama was willing to pay planters $30 a month for each slave sent to work on the defenses around Mobile. Nonetheless, most planters continued to thwart the use of slave labor throughout the War. "Patriotic planters would willingly put their own flesh and blood into the army," recalled Senator Louis T. Wigfall of Texas, but when "you asked them for a negro," it was like "drawing an eyetooth."

Nevertheless, the Ordnance Bureau by 1863 was supplying all the small arms and ammunition the Army could use. Josiah Gorgas wrote in his diary that he had succeeded "beyond my utmost expectations." He prided himself on the fact that less than

three years after the start of the War, the Confederate armies never lost a major battle because of lack of armaments — and that on some occasions they were better equipped than the Federals.

Southern industry was less successful at clothing Confederate troops. There were a number of reasons for this, one of which was the inadequacy of the Confederate Quartermaster Department under Colonel Abraham C. Myers. Although he was a West Pointer and an experienced supply officer, Myers was soon overwhelmed by the difficulties he faced.

In the summer of 1861, for example, Colonel Myers set up a large factory in Richmond that was responsible for cutting the cloth for uniforms but not for producing the finished product. He entrusted the sewing to local women, who did the work in their homes. Soon there were 2,000 women stitching uniforms in Richmond, another 3,000 in Atlanta and thousands more working throughout the South. This decentralized cottage industry was highly dependent on transport — and the South's fragile railroad system was never equal to the task. As a result, military uniforms remained in short supply.

Compounding the problems caused by poor planning in Richmond was the fact that individual states often reserved most of the cotton and wool produced within their borders for men of their own militias. This practice left little cloth for the Confederate troops. At the end of 1864, North Carolina was consuming the entire production of her 40 textile mills — fully half of the mills remaining in the South.

Efforts to supply the troops with shoes were no more successful. Raw leather had been scarce in a region accustomed to buying its shoes and saddles from the North. However, the Confederacy had expected to get what it needed from the cattle and horse farms and nascent tanneries of Tennessee. When that source was cut off by invasion in 1862, the South faced a chronic shortage of leather.

President Davis finally dismissed Myers in 1863, but by then the outfitting of the Army had become hopelessly snarled. In the autumn of that year, Confederate War Department Chief Robert Kean noted in his diary that the Quartermaster Department had provided no shoes for nearly a year. Lee's army, he added, was going barefoot.

In coping with wartime shortages, independent entrepreneurs often showed more flexibility than did the government bureaucracy or the military agencies. Cobblers experimented with the skins of squirrels, alligators and even dogs, and sold as many wooden clogs as they could make. Joseph A. Turner, a planter and newspaper editor from Putnam County, Georgia, advertised hats made from the pelts of rabbits, racoons, "and all other skins that have fur on them." Cottage industries sprang up to make ladies' bonnets fashioned from pine needles, palmetto fronds, straw and corn shucks.

Hundreds of patents were issued during the War — most of them for agricultural inventions such as new plows, hoes, seed planters and cotton cleaners. Southerners took great pride in manufacturing goods traditionally obtained from the North, or in devising substitutes for them. Lead pencils purported to be "as good as Faber's" were made in Greensboro, Alabama. A merchant in Jackson, Mississippi, proudly announced that he had "Rebel Matches" in stock; among the first friction matches ever manu-

THE LOVELY LIZZIE
Transports all the MALES in the Confederacy free of charge and with astonishing celerity!

factured in the Confederacy, they were guaranteed by the maker to be better than the Northern variety. The newspapers extolled the remarkable properties of new machines — such as the marvel of a shoe-peg factory in Staunton, Virginia, that was said to be able to convert a maple tree into pegs before a stammering man could say "Jack Robinson."

The increase in industrial activity, both civilian and military, put an enormous strain on the South's transportation system, particularly the railroads. Designed primarily to move staple crops over relatively short distances, the rail network proved entirely unsuited to war. There were only 9,000 miles of track in the whole of the South, compared to 22,000 miles in the North. Moreover, the system was divided between 113 small railroads — the largest of which owned only 469 miles of track, while the smallest were characterized by one wit as little more than "a right-of-way and two streaks of rust."

Worse yet was the problem of track width: Most Southern railroads used a standard

A pun-filled valentine to a Southern woman praises the speed of the fictitious train "Lovely Lizzie." In contrast, real Southern railways were cheaply built and unreliable. "Unless some improvement is made," complained General Robert E. Lee to President Davis in 1864, "I do not know what will become of us."

Mules haul a wagon loaded with firewood across a brook in Virginia. Under Confederate law of impressment, citizens were obliged to sell the Army their best wagons, horses and mules, and had to make do with whatever means of transportation remained.

five-foot gauge, but vital rail lines in Virginia and North Carolina had a gauge of four feet eight and one half inches. This produced serious delays in moving supplies from the deep South to the Virginia front or from Richmond to other cities. Beyond the Mississippi River, the gauges were even less consistent, ranging from five and a half feet to four feet eight inches.

In addition, at important rail centers such as Richmond, Augusta and Savannah, the railroads did not connect. This meant that freight had to be unloaded, transported across the city by wagon and then reloaded onto another train.

Greater gaps elsewhere in the system turned what could have been simple trips into marathons. To get from Jackson, Mississippi, to the first Confederate capital at Montgomery, Alabama, for his inauguration, Jefferson Davis had to make a roundabout journey of 750 miles via Chattanooga, instead of the 250 miles he would have traveled had the rail network not lacked a vital link between Selma and Montgomery.

Davis asked for and got a million-dollar appropriation to close the most critical gap in the Southern rail network — a 40-mile stretch between Greensboro, North Carolina, and Danville, Virginia. But some Con-

federate leaders protested that the Davis plan was a violation of states' rights. A Richmond newspaper editorial warned: "The precedent of government aid to railroads is dangerous, and liable to abuses and corruptions." North Carolina Governor Zebulon Baird Vance opposed the link because he feared that it would take commerce from local lines. Planters along the proposed route refused to let their slaves work on it. As a result, a project that should have taken six months took over two years.

Under such conditions, it was not uncommon for men and equipment en route to the battlefield to be delayed for days, or for freight to pile up for weeks. Yet the rail companies were too blindly competitive to listen to government pleas that they agree upon a standard rail gauge, join their lines at important terminals and lend one another rolling stock.

Most of the equipment of the Southern railroads became so decrepit that a train's average speed was only about 12 miles an hour, even in the best of circumstances. Lack of fuel supplies forced engineers to stop frequently while the crew gathered wood. Moreover, since most railroads were single-track, trains had to pull off on sidings to permit passage of traffic in the opposite direction. In 1862, one soldier took eight weary days, his train sitting at length on sidings, to travel from Manassas, Virginia, to Augusta, Georgia.

At each regular station, the few available trains were nearly buried under swarms of passengers — a spectacle compared by one Confederate officer to "what you see when you throw a stick into a beehive." A seat with an intact bottom or back was a rare luxury. Cars generally lacked windows, lamps, heat

INDIAN COTTON DEPÔT

OVER THE WAY.

Mr. Bull. "OH! IF YOU TWO LIKE FIGHTING BETTER THAN BUSINESS, I SHALL DEAL AT THE OTHER SHOP."

Spurning the squabbling Americans in this British cartoon, a plump John Bull, the symbol of Great Britain, ponders purchasing his cotton from an eager Indian. Although Indian cotton was inferior to the American variety, it eased Britain's so-called cotton famine, produced by the self-imposed Confederate embargo.

and drinking water. As parts wore out and roadbeds deteriorated, accidents became frequent. One traveler, Sir Arthur Fremantle, a British lieutenant colonel observing the Confederate Army, was barely five miles outside Jackson, Mississippi, when the engine of his train ran off the track, turning his 50-mile trip to Meridian, Mississippi, into a 16-hour grind.

The one thing that might have salvaged a system so starved for labor and materials was a takeover by the government — but this the Davis administration was not prepared to do until the last days of the conflict. By makeshift devices — cannibalizing branch lines to repair essential lines, for example — a Southern rail network was kept open. But it served Confederate industry less and less well. By 1864 the Tredegar Works in Richmond could no longer obtain raw iron from Alabama because the railroads were unable to deliver it.

The situation might have proved less serious had other forms of transport functioned adequately. But the entire Southern transportation system was in trouble. The Union's coastal blockade and Federal control of major rivers in the South severely restricted Confederate water traffic.

Wagons, together with mules and horses to pull them, grew increasingly scarce as the murderous toll of animals and the wreckage of equipment mounted on the battlefields. In its desperate search for replacements, the government resorted more and more frequently to seizure of animals and wagons under the impressment laws. Notorious for paying a fraction of market prices — or sometimes nothing at all — the "pressmen," as the Confederate agents were known, stirred a storm of bitterness. For a time, people had to make do by using sleds and crude two-wheel carts that they hitched to oxen or cows. Even so, impressment did not solve the government's transportation problem. As the Federal grip on the Mississippi River tightened, cutting off the supply of horses and mules from Texas, many of the wagon routes that served as feeders to the railroad arteries were virtually abandoned.

The Confederacy suffered from another major deficiency — a shortage of food. Because so much acreage was devoted to cotton and other staple crops, parts of the plantation South had relied on the farms of the upper Mississippi Valley for many essentials in its diet. Beef, pork, corn, flour, fruits, butter, cheese — all had come by steamboat and rail from states now in the Union.

In 1862, the Confederate Congress adopted a resolution urging that food crops be planted instead of cotton and tobacco. Several states went further and passed laws forbidding any farmer to plant more than two bales of cotton per field hand. "Plant corn and be free, or plant cotton and be whipped!" cried the Columbus, Georgia, *Sun*. Corn and patriotism became synonymous, and planters of cotton were held up to scorn. "O, that every planter could realize the immeasurable amount of mischief which the devil can sow in only four acres of cotton!" exclaimed the Macon *Daily Telegraph*. In a special effort to ensure that grain crops went for food, most states suppressed whiskey-making, forbidding the distillation of alcohol from corn, wheat or other grains.

Some planters defied the tide of opinion and argued that the more cotton planted the better — since cotton stores could be hoarded and used as a diplomatic lever in the South's behalf. At the beginning of the War the South placed an embargo on its own cotton, on the theory that English manufacturers, idled by lack of the fiber, would pressure the British government to recognize the Confederacy. The theory proved insubstantial, of course — the scheme had no effect in the long run. And for the most part, the South turned from cotton to corn with extraordinary energy.

The cotton harvest, which had amounted to 4.5 million bales in 1861, dropped in each successive year until it stood at 300,000 bales in 1864. Jefferson Davis proudly told Congress that all over the South, cereals were growing in "fields no longer whitened by cotton." General William Tecumseh Sherman, finding food and forage abundant on his march through Georgia, added his own wry tribute. "Convey to Jeff Davis," he wrote, "my personal and official thanks for abolishing cotton and substituting corn and sweet potatoes."

Reviewing the South's prodigious efforts to feed itself, a supply officer remarked in 1863 that "our battle against want and starvation is greater than against our enemies." Oddly, it was a battle that the South both won and lost. Unquestionably, the South managed to raise more than enough food to sustain the entire population. But often the food failed to reach either civilians in the cities or soldiers on the battlefields. Thus, while Lee's army was going hungry and city dwellers were feeling the threat of famine, food was rotting on loading platforms or railroad sidings.

Food that did reach the market was so expensive that most families were hard-pressed to buy staples. In the winter of 1864, for example, Richmond's John Beauchamp Jones was earning a respectable $3,000 a year, but he wondered "what income would suffice" to pay the prevailing prices: bacon, $9 a pound; turnip greens, $4 a peck; flour, $275 a barrel; potatoes, $25 a bushel. "I saw a *ham* sell today for $350," wrote Jones. Six weeks later he noted that he could not scrape up money for more than an ounce of meat daily for each member of his family.

Elsewhere in the city, citizens attacked a Baptist preacher for selling flour at $500 a barrel and meal for $100 a bushel. According to a wry joke making the rounds, shoppers took their money to the market in bushel baskets and returned with their purchases in their pocketbooks.

Public opinion blamed the inflation on the government's fiscal policy — or lack of it.

Southern author and diarist Mary Chesnut, shown in an 1850s portrait, was married to a wealthy Confederate Army officer. Many times during the War she rose at dawn to work at a nearby hospital, and she was openly critical of those who refused to make sacrifices for the war effort: "Time is coming when they will not be given a choice," she prophesied.

The man responsible for Confederate finance was Secretary of Treasury Christopher G. Memminger, who had been a successful lawyer in Charleston. He began Treasury operations in a bare, unswept room in Montgomery, without paper, chair or desk. Fortunately, the fledgling Treasury was not totally without funds, for it had just accepted from Alabama a loan of $500,000 and another from Louisiana of the same amount in specie seized from the Federal customhouse and mint in New Orleans.

Memminger's initial mistake was to assume that the War would not last long and that he could treat the financial needs of the Confederacy as he would those of a young nation at peace. He called for a few minor war taxes and a modest bond issue — reasoning that the government could pay for a brief war with I.O.U.s and then erase those debts with taxation and import duties in peacetime.

This lack of foresight also led Memminger to rely too much on import duties in the expectation that the Confederacy's foreign trade would continue unabated. Import duties did bring in $3.5 million during the War. But most of this was collected before the Federal blockade took effect, at which point the Confederacy's overseas trade virtually disappeared.

Bonds, too, were productive sources of income early in the War, when secessionist fever ran high. By the late fall of 1861, bonds had brought the Confederacy $15 million in specie. But sales soon fell off, and continued to slide until the government was forced to offer bonds that could be purchased with farm produce rather than cash, which was becoming increasingly scarce. The Treasury thus acquired vast stores of cotton and tobac-

co—almost none of which could be sold to Europe and thereby converted into cash.

In all, the Confederate Treasury amassed $27 million in specie, most of it obtained from the initial sale of bonds and from the seizure of funds in Federal customhouses and Northern-controlled banks in the South. Almost all of this specie went to Europe to pay for war goods. Now Memminger faced a dilemma: The Treasury had no money to pay its future bills, and the people, meanwhile, had no national medium of exchange. Instead of trying to increase the cash supply by more rigorous taxation, Memminger made the disastrous decision to issue paper money

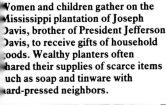

Women and children gather on the Mississippi plantation of Joseph Davis, brother of President Jefferson Davis, to receive gifts of household goods. Wealthy planters often shared their supplies of scarce items such as soap and tinware with hard-pressed neighbors.

31

After the Federal capture of Port Royal in November 1861, Confederate soldiers and civilians at nearby Beaufort, South Carolina, burn cotton to prevent it from falling into enemy hands. During four years of war, advancing Federal armies forced the South to destroy an estimated 2.5 million bales.

unsupported by gold. Congress authorized Memminger's plan for an initial printing of $100 million in notes. Women in Richmond were paid $500 a year to sit as clerks in the Treasury signing their names to the bills as they came off the presses — a device Memminger had conceived because he thought, incorrectly, that the multiplicity of signatures would make the notes more difficult to counterfeit.

Lacking die cutters, the Confederacy failed to coin its own money. Instead, the Treasury announced that United States silver coins — along with English sovereigns, French Napoleons, and Spanish and Mexican doubloons — would be considered legal tender with fixed values established by the government. In addition, the Treasury issued small paper notes derisively known as shinplasters, in denominations from five to 50 cents, to facilitate the making of change. Within weeks, individuals were cranking out unauthorized shinplasters by the thousands. "Great God, what a people!" exclaimed a Mississippi editor. "Two hundred and fifty different sorts of shinplasters and not one dime in silver to be seen!"

To add to the confusion, United States greenbacks brought in by the invading armies and by prisoners of war began circulating in the South in 1863; these notes were valued at a premium of 4 to 1 over Confederate money. Moreover, the Southern states issued large amounts of their own currency and permitted cities, railroads and insurance companies to issue bills in their own names. Finally, enterprising Northerners printed and dumped carloads of phony Confederate bills to debase further the South's currency. All told, an estimated $2.2 billion in paper money was floating around in the Confederacy.

In the spring of 1863 the alarmed Confederate Congress finally passed a law taxing income and property on a scale varying from 1 per cent of incomes less than $1,000 to 15 per cent of incomes over $10,000. But the remedy came far too late to halt the dizzying inflationary spiral. Prices were rising at an almost constant rate of 10 per cent a month. Officers' uniforms by 1864 were selling for $2,000 and shoes for from $200 to $800 a pair. Currency at last became so worthless that much daily business was carried on by barter — two bushels of salt for a pair of shoes, five turkeys for a bonnet, a quantity of bacon and potatoes for board and tuition at school.

Although the government in Richmond was widely blamed for runaway inflation, it was not entirely responsible. The real shortage of consumer goods contributed as much to inflation as the surplus of cash. And the government had little control over speculators, or the disruption of the Confederacy's foreign trade by blockade — or the chaotic effects of Federal invasion, which steadily reduced the taxable population. Yet many in the South shared the opinion of diarist Mary Chesnut, who wrote that "the Confederacy has been done to death by the politicians."

Indeed, politicians of all stripes were regarded with increasing disdain as the War went on. To a nation in rapid flux, the activities of the Congressmen and bureaucrats in Richmond seemed less and less helpful. Events had outstripped the planners, and nobody caught in the turmoil dared predict what kind of society would emerge.

Hectic Days in the Capital

Confederate troops and artillery approach Richmond early in the War. Space in the city was at such a premium that cavalry officers had to be quartered at a raceco

After Richmond was named the Confederate capital in May 1861, the city was besieged by an army of Southern outlanders. Politicians, military leaders, government workers and their families all swarmed into the once-quiet town, swelling the prewar population of 38,000. This influx was soon followed by droves of soldiers converging from all parts of the Confederacy. "Every hour there are arrivals of organized companies from the country," wrote a clerk in the War Department. "The precincts of the city will soon be a series of encampments."

With the soldiers came a host of characters who cared little for the Confederate cause. Profiteers, counterfeiters, pickpockets and spies descended in force upon the city, and for a time the police were powerless to restrain them.

The inundation continued as Richmond absorbed countless victims of the War. In time, the city was filled to overflowing with wounded soldiers, Federal prisoners and uprooted civilians.

Exultant Richmonders gather at the Capitol for a 100-gun salute to celebrate the victory at Manassas in July 1861. Said one resident, "The city seemed lifted up, and everyone appeared to walk on air."

Recruiting for the Army, a fife-and-drum band parades along a sidewalk in front of Richmond's Exchange Hotel in May 1861. By fall, nearly three fourths of the city's 4,000 young men had enlisted.

In one of Richmond's fashionable districts, residents and their household servants

The War Brought Home

Richmond residents greeted the news of early Confederate victories with jubilation. As the fighting neared the capital, however, the realities of war cast a pall of gloom over the citizenry.

In June 1862, after the Battle of Seven Pines, nearly 5,000 casualties had to be cared for in the capital. Bandaged and bleeding soldiers were carried into town on litters, carts and railroad flatcars. "Almost every house in the city was a private hospital," reported Richmonder Sallie Brock, "and almost every woman a nurse."

Still, Richmond's resources fell far short of the task, and hundreds of men died simply because their wounds went unattended.

...ister to Confederate troops wounded at Seven Pines. Diarist Mary Chesnut described the victims as "awfully smashed-up objects of misery."

Eager to glimpse "Lincoln's hirelings," as Federal soldiers were called, curiosity-seekers crowd into a Richmond hospital ward filled with wounded prisoners. Said captive William Merrell, "Hardly were the prisoners comfortably bestowed in hospital quarters, before the place literally swarmed with visitors."

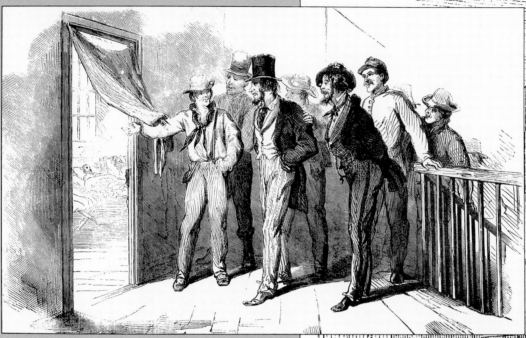

The Captors' Burden

"Every train brings in a fresh batch of these Abolition jewels to be fed and cared for at Government expense," wrote a Richmond reporter of Federal prisoners in 1863. Indeed, that year as many as 4,000 captured officers were crowded into hastily converted tobacco warehouses along the James River, and the number of enlisted men confined in tents on nearby Belle Isle eventually grew to 10,000.

Richmond residents fretted constantly about the prospect of a mass escape by the prisoners. Worse, the Federals' presence sapped the city's dwindling food supply, adding to the anxiety of the townspeople.

Federal prisoners of war fling their tattered uniforms from the windows of a tobacco wareho

re they were housed, to slaves waiting below in February 1862. The soldiers, due to be exchanged soon for Confederate prisoners, had just received new clothing.

Flight to the City

For thousands of Southerners, Richmond became a city of refuge. Runaway slaves, destitute soldiers' wives and Army deserters all flocked to the capital, along with loyalists ejected from Federal-occupied zones for refusing to swear allegiance to the Union. One such exile was Constance Harrison, whose family could find no better lodgings than a "dismal rookery crowded with its limits with refugees like ourselves."

Largely as a result of this migration rents increased fourfold in just two years and by 1864 the city's population had more than trebled to 128,000. Richmond, remarked Mary Chesnut, had filled "to suffocation — hardly standing room left."

Rocketts Landing on the James River near Richmond received thousands of homeless civilians fleeing the battle zones. Following a long and fruitless search for sh

the teeming capital, one new arrival lamented: "Have returned fatigued and hopeless. I do not believe there is a vacant spot in the city."

A Culture Transformed

"There are nights here with the moonlight cold and ghostly when I could tear my hair & cry aloud for all that is past & gone."

MARY BOYKIN CHESNUT

The changes came gradually at first. For a time after the outbreak of war, the small towns still slumbered. Around courthouse squares, old men still sat tilted back in chairs, gossiping and spitting tobacco juice while they took in all that passed before them. In the fields, the lean, worn farmers still worked exhausting hours—from dawn until sunset—behind their teams of mules.

On the large plantations, it was almost possible to pretend that the South was not at war. When Charles Colcock Jones Jr. of Georgia went off to join the Confederate Army in the autumn of 1861, life on his family's plantation was much as always. Jones later described that life as an "ample" existence, presenting "no lack of service" of any description.

"These were generous homes," Jones wrote, "and the hospitality there extended was profuse and refined." An extensive staff of slaves maintained the high standards of the household. "Daddy Jack was the major-domo," Jones remembered. "Patience and Lucy were the chambermaids. Phoebe and Clarissa were the seamstresses. Marcia was the cook. Gilbert was the carriage driver. Flora and Silvy were the handmaidens. Jupiter and Caesar were the gardeners, and sundry younger servants were commissioned to sweep, scrub, and run on errands. Niger was the fisherman, and there was a lad to bring the triweekly mail."

Thus cossetted, the Jones family moved back and forth between its winter plantations, Arcadia and Montevideo, and its coastal plantation, Maybank, which afforded cooling sea breezes in summer. The boys of such families often studied with private tutors, hunted and fished, and rode with neighborhood children in what Jones described as "a little cavalry company," formed "that we might be encouraged in the art of riding and swordsmanship." The girls usually practiced "the ornamentals"—French, piano playing, singing, drawing and painting.

That genteel way of life was inexorably altered by the tide of war. Not only were the planters affected: Southerners of all walks of life saw their cultural institutions and social traditions turned upside down in the course of the conflict.

Poets and writers, inspired by patriotic themes, flourished as never before. Yet at the same time, schools closed for lack of teachers and universities for lack of students. Clergymen turned from God's work and instead used their pulpits to preach a fiery gospel of propaganda for the Confederate cause. Through it all, the class lines that had been so much a part of Southern life proceeded to give way, and women suddenly found themselves rising to levels of responsibility undreamed of in the past.

When the fighting started, many plantation owners and their sons were quick to join the military. "Let the gentlemen set the example," declared a South Carolina Senator,

The pattern of the outlawed Confederate national flag, the Stars and Bars, is ingeniously disguised in this faded lithograph of Southern flowers made during the Federal occupation of New Orleans by a local drawing instructor. The small white flowers among the blue blossoms represent the flag's stars; the darker lateral fringes are its bars. The bold deception was soon spotted by Federal authorities, who destroyed all but a handful of the prints.

in a burst of patriotic fervor. "Let them go in the ranks."

The women were left behind to wait and to worry. No matter how far away the actual fighting might be, plantation mistresses found the War impinging on their consciousness, even as they cultivated their tuberoses and dahlias or sat down to read verse with their friends. "The time for poetry is past," wrote Catherine Ann Edmondston on her plantation in eastern North Carolina in 1861. The War was so oppressively on her mind, she recorded, that whenever she turned the page of a book she could not remember "what was on the other side."

As happened elsewhere in the South, her plantation's teams and wagons were soon requisitioned — along with a fourth of the able-bodied men — for work on fortifications. As the threat of invasion grew, the silverware, fine brandy and precious books were shipped off to a place of safety, and the plantation's signal bells were donated to the Confederacy, to be melted down for cannon. "Ladies who never worked before," noted Catherine Edmondston in her diary, "are hard at work making uniforms and tents."

Such women felt a sense of deep personal involvement in the War partly because planter society resembled a huge, extended family. When Mary Chesnut noted despairingly in May of 1864 that "the dreadful work of death is beginning again," she was referring not only to the death of a favorite cousin at the head of his regiment but also to the fact that virtually every day's casualty lists contained the names of distant relatives or family friends.

Marriage, remarriage and intermarriage had created extensive and sometimes bewildering ties that connected members of enor-

mous tribes by blood and a sense of fidelity. These family networks were deeply rooted. In the early decades of the 19th Century, for example, the prosperous planter Captain Joseph Jones of the Georgia coast had 26 children by three wives. By the time of the Civil War, the family in all its sundry branches could be found not only in Georgia but across the South. The family included hundreds of kinsmen who were in frequent touch with one another.

It was common for first cousins to marry, or for two brothers in one family to marry two sisters in another. In one district of Alabama, 38 per cent of slaveholding couples were first cousins. The pattern was no less pronounced among plain folk. An illiterate Alabama farmer had 17 children and eventually became the patriarch of a clan of 234 descendants in a single community.

The kinship ties could span great distances and leap across class lines. The war diary of Sarah Morgan, daughter of a judge in Louisiana, contains many of the same names as Mary Chesnut's journals, for the two women were related by blood or by marriage to the same families, even though they were not personally acquainted and were separated by a thousand miles. And although there seemed to be little in common between the great slaveholders and the simple farmers living in their "dog-run" cabins on a hog-and-corn economy, the fact was that a number of plantation owners had risen from the ranks of farmers and still had relatives there.

As on the plantations, life on small farms and in rural towns began to change noticeably as the Confederacy became more deeply involved in the War. Male clerks disappeared from the stores, and so many medical

Southern women enjoy a peaceful
moment with their sewing under the
trees on Cedar Mountain in Virginia.
As supplies of cloth dwindled and
clothing wore out, such domestic
handiwork became essential.

men went off to war that some areas were left
without care. Women were forced to run
farms with the help only of old people and
children. To make matters worse, the farms
ran short of tools and implements — for it
was all but impossible to replace the metal
parts of plows, wagons, hoes and scythes.
Families had to rely on whatever makeshift
implements they could find or devise to
work their fields. Many simply gave up the
struggle and attempted to feed their families
on the paltry relief funds doled out by some
state governments.

Amid the social upheaval brought by the
War there were new opportunities for literary and artistic talents that had languished in
the torpid antebellum years. The Confederate crusade furnished an apparently inexhaustible theme in the exaltation of the
South and its ideals. Indeed, the rapturous
Sidney Lanier welcomed the conflict as
the seedbed of a new Southern literature.
An editor in Richmond declared the dis-
tinguishing color of that new literature to
be "not rose-pink but blood-red," its per-
fume "that of sulphur and nitre," its sound
the "ring of steel."

Many Southern writers prospered during
the War as they never had in time of peace.
The South Carolina novelist William Gil-
more Simms switched from writing obscure
romances to the more profitable genre of
pamphleteering for the South — agreeing
with Sidney Lanier that literary men had an
obligation to sustain public morale and defend Southern rights.

Augusta Jane Evans of Alabama, a well-
known writer before the War, produced a
novel called *Macaria; or, Altars of Sacrifice*,
which incorporated a report of the Battle

of Bull Run sent to her by General Beauregard. Writing in a sentimental and moralistic tone, Miss Evans dedicated her book to "the Brave Soldiers of the Southern Army." By the time it had gone through two editions, she was famous.

Almost equally popular was John Esten Cooke, a Virginia lawyer and devoted exponent of the theory that Virginians were descended from the aristocratic, English Cavaliers who migrated to America in the mid-17th Century. "Where are they now, those stalwart cavaliers and lovely dames?" Cooke asked in one of his early novels. He repeated the question, or something like it, in book after book, all of which sold briskly. His wartime popularity received a special boost from his worshipful *The Life of Stonewall Jackson,* published in 1863. This biography argued the merits of the Confederate cause so passionately that Federal authorities in Kentucky succeeded in having the book banned in the state.

Although the Federal blockade isolated the Confederate States from the books of European publishers, presses throughout the South contrived to print smuggled editions of some of the Continent's more popular works. Victor Hugo's *Les Misérables*—from which the passages condemning slavery were carefully excised—sold better than any other foreign book throughout the War. There was also an apparently inexhaustible audience for the medieval romances of Sir Walter Scott—who had so filled the Southern imagination with "sham chivalries," wrote Mark Twain, that he must be held "in a great measure responsible for the war." It was not just civilians who were enthralled by Scott: A Confederate soldier, John Green of Kentucky, complained in his diary about the difficulty of sitting in a rifle pit outside Atlanta and trying to read aloud from Scott's *The Heart of Midlothian* over the crash of Federal guns.

Poetry, too, enjoyed a surge of popularity. Paul Hamilton Hayne, a wellborn Charlestonian, penned verse inspired by the military triumphs of Stonewall Jackson and John Hunt Morgan, and paid poetic tribute to the defenders of Vicksburg and Charleston. "The poetic vein is at flood-tide," he exulted to his wife in the spring of 1862.

Dedicated Virginians could recite from memory "The Sword of Robert E. Lee," written with great passion by a Confederate chaplain named Abram Joseph Ryan. Other poems, such as George Bagby's "The Empty Sleeve," and the anonymous ballad "When This Cruel War Is Over," spoke of sorrows many Confederate families had experienced at first hand. Francis Ticknor's "Virginians of the Valley," on the other hand, embraced the chivalric theme by describing the Virginia soldier as "The Knightliest of the Knightly race / That since the days of old / Have kept the lamp of chivalry / Alight in hearts of gold."

Perhaps the most popular poet in the South was South Carolina's Henry Timrod, who was known to his admirers as the "poet laureate of the Confederacy." A former schoolteacher, Timrod was so exhilarated by the birth of the Confederacy that he quickly wrote two celebrations, one entitled "Ethnogenesis" and the other "The Cotton Boll," in which he rhapsodized that "since the world began / No fairer land hath fired a poet's lays / Or given a home to man!"

As the War went on, however, Timrod gradually became depressed, and his poetry reflected the increasingly bleak mood of the

The Fruits of Patriotic Pastimes

Many Southern women expressed their devotion to the Confederate cause by spending leisure hours fashioning articles with patriotic motifs. Scarves, cockades, dresses and flags were the most common examples of their prodigious craftsmanship.

MINIATURE FLAG AND PATRIOTIC POEM

CHILD'S DRESS WITH SASH

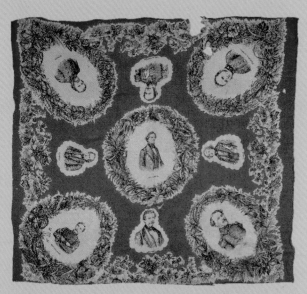

SCARF DECORATED WITH CONFEDERATE PORTRAITS

FLAG OF PAPER ROSES

South. On a dreary winter's day, with "the rain plashing on my sill," he wrote of "The Unknown Dead" lying beneath Southern hills. In his poem "Christmas," which was written shortly before the close of the War and his own death from tuberculosis, there was no trace of his early exuberance; he could think only of uttering "a prayer whose theme is — peace."

Passionate amateurs by the hundreds flooded newspapers and other periodicals with unsolicited contributions bearing titles as diverse as "South Carolina's Justification to the North" and "The Devil's Visit to Old Abe." Some newspaper editors tried to stem the tide by charging contributors 10 cents a line for anything printed. Others stopped publishing poetry entirely. George Bagby, a poet and editor of the distinguished *Southern Literary Messenger*, used his "Editor's Table" column in July 1863 to plead with his avid readers not to send "too much trash in rhyme." It was summertime, he explained with mock severity, and he did not want to fire up his office stove to burn the piles of contributions. As for tearing up poetry and throwing it out the window, he deemed that totally useless: "The vexatious wind always blows it back."

Tiresome though it may have been, bad poetry was the least of the problems a Southern editor faced in wartime. Far more pressing was the extreme shortage of newsprint. Cut off from their usual suppliers in the North, editors were forced to tailor the size of their publications to the fluctuating paper allocations they got from local mills. As a result, observed the *Confederate States Almanac* for 1863, a paper might be "short enough for a pocket handkerchief one day and big enough for a tablecloth another."

When the supply of white paper ran out, editors resorted to printing on any color paper they could find — producing issues, noted the *Almanac*, with "as many hues as Niagara in the sunshine." Subscribers to the Charleston *Mercury* received their news on a fuchsia background, which faded on occasion to a dusty salmon. Houston's *Tri-Weekly Telegraph* appeared in brown, shell pink, orange, moss green, kelly green, blue and yellow. Editions of the Vicksburg *Daily Citizen* were printed on the blank side of wallpaper. As the besieged city fell to General Ulysses S. Grant in 1863, the editors wryly expressed regret that their readers might no longer have the benefit of the colorful "wallpaper edition."

Inflation and an uncertain postal service further complicated newspaper operations. Ink was so scarce that one resourceful paper, the Memphis *Appeal*, used shoe polish to blacken the type. Other newspapers, in a desperate effort to hold their financially bereft readership, offered to accept payment for subscriptions in barter. The Athens *Southern Watchman* informed its readers in 1861 that they could settle their accounts in corn, butter, shucks, hay or chicken — in fact, in "anything that can be eaten or worn, or that will answer for fuel."

Despite such emergency measures, Southern newspapers were decimated. In Florida, 17 of 26 papers ceased publication during the first year of the War. Only 26 of 57 in North Carolina survived the conflict. Virginia lost 86 per cent of its papers. One Virginia paper told its readers in the spring of 1862 that it was going out of business for lack of editors, compositors, printers, paper and ink, and concluded: "The devil only is left in the office."

The publications that survived were not only hardy but fiercely independent. Although they had nearly unanimously endorsed secession, a number of papers became bitter critics of the Davis government. Most of the five Richmond dailies — with the *Examiner* in the lead — persistently attacked the President's Cabinet appointments. Papers in Lynchburg and Raleigh, Augusta and Charles Town also heaped abuse on the President. One newspaper even blamed Davis for the fact that Confederate soldiers marched in the snow without shoes.

Despite such bitter attacks, Davis and his government remained resolutely loyal to the principle of a free press, tolerating newspaper criticism with amazing patience. When British Lieutenant Colonel Arthur Fremantle toured the American continent in 1863, he fully expected to find that freedom of the press had been sharply curtailed in the slaveholding South. Instead, he discovered that the most violent editorial attacks upon the Confederate President and his generals were permitted to pass without official challenge.

There were censorship laws and Confederate military decrees against publishing news on troop concentrations and movements, but these edicts had little restraining influence on the press. Editors felt it their right, and even their duty, to print plans of campaigns, detailed information about troops, the departure dates of blockade runners, the size and location of war industries. So precise was some of this information that Mary Chesnut concluded the North required no spies — for "our own newspapers tell ev-

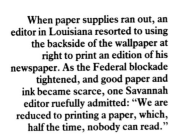

...idents of New Bern, North ...olina, gather at the stationer's ...e to follow the progress of the ...through the latest newspapers ...magazines. The town was ...er Federal occupation from ...ch 1862 until the end of the War.

When paper supplies ran out, an editor in Louisiana resorted to using the backside of the wallpaper at right to print an edition of his newspaper. As the Federal blockade tightened, and good paper and ink became scarce, one Savannah editor ruefully admitted: "We are reduced to printing a paper, which, half the time, nobody can read."

ery word there is to be told by friend or foe." As the war news worsened, the lack of censorship undoubtedly contributed to the deterioration of civilian morale and the loss of a will to fight.

Yet, paradoxically, the press also strived to be a builder of morale. Alongside their political vituperations, papers ran marathon commentaries specifically designed to buoy Southern hopes. Against all evidence, editorial writers insisted that Northerners could not fight: "Their most bloodthirsty achievements," said the New Orleans *Crescent,* "consist of harpooning whales and eviscerating codfish." The New Orleans *Bee* never recognized Shiloh as a Confederate reverse. To take Vicksburg had cost the Yankees 100,000 men, said the *South Carolinian* — and what good would the Mississippi do

them? Some papers treated Gettysburg as a Southern triumph three weeks after Lee retreated into Virginia.

Newspapers also tried to boost morale with humorous tales and vignettes, which had always been traditional staples of the small-town Southern press. Most successful of the wartime humorists was Charles Henry Smith of Rome, Georgia. While serving in the Confederate Army in 1861, Smith began sending letters to the Rome *Confederation* addressed to "Mr. Abe Linkhorn" and signed "Bill Arp."

In the letters Smith, as "Arp," assumed the role of a good-natured Southern bumpkin recalling nostalgically the simple pleasures of the farm and ridiculing the human frailties exposed by the War. Profiteers were favorite targets, but he also made fun of the bumbling Georgia militia and the fiery patriots who suddenly became crippled rheumatics when a general conscription law was passed. The Bill Arp letters soon became so popular that they were picked up by other newspapers and eventually published in book form.

A somewhat similar but more bitterly satirical comic character was the Tennessee bumpkin known to newspaper readers as Sut Lovingood. This oafish spinner of yarns was a mouthpiece for the Tennessee journalist George Washington Harris. Speaking a sort of poor-white dialect — "naik" for "neck," for example, and "hit" for "it" — Sut launched vicious diatribes against not only blacks and Yankees, but also small-town merchants and anyone else who had risen out of the poor-white class. The humor, in the crude and sometimes brutal tradition of the American frontier, consisted largely of prac-tical jokes played by Sut on his real or imagined enemies. The sketches became increasingly popular as war pressures mounted and more people began to feel the kinds of frustrations and social resentments that Sut Lovingood openly expressed.

The desire for comic diversion led publishers to paste together a multitude of war-joke books with such titles as *The Camp Jester; or, Amusement for the Mess* and *Ups and Downs of Wife Hunting, or Merry Jokes for Camp Perusal*. Just as popular were the more than 600 pieces of sentimental sheet music that celebrated the heroism or pathos of the Confederate cause. Some of these songs — "The Bonnie Blue Flag" and "Stonewall Jackson's Way" — survived the War. Others, such as "The Manassas Quickstep," would vanish along with the Confederacy. Dirges, not surprisingly, were widespread. The death of Stonewall Jackson precipi-

An elderly planter gathers his kin to cheer Confederate troops marching off to Chickamauga. Published in a Georgia periodical, this drawing carried the inspiring caption: "Yes, my children; there they come, our country's deliverers. We are now safe from the tyrant invader."

Shade trees festooned with Spanish moss line a walk leading to the plantation home of Robert Barnwell Rhett Jr. *(inset)*, influential editor of the Charleston, South Carolina, *Mercury*. A bitter critic of Jefferson Davis, Rhett once referred to the Confederate President as "this little head of a great country."

tated a slew of songs mourning his loss.

A particular favorite among the soldiers was a sad ballad called "Lorena." A friend of Mary Chesnut speculated that "a girl in large hoops and a calico frock" was seated "at every piano between Richmond and the Mississippi," stumbling through "Lorena" while gazing up soulfully into the eyes of a Confederate soldier.

The professional stage hatched a good share of these popular songs, including the celebrated "Battle of Manassas," composed, sung and played on the piano with suitable crescendos by a Georgia slave named Blind Tom. Like many another performer, he benefited from the boom in theatrical activity that followed the wartime migration to the cities. Audiences hungry for diversion crowded into playhouses to see minstrel shows, Shakespearean drama or farces such as *King Linkum, the First,* and *The Royal Ape,* both of which lampooned the hated Yankee President.

Staid old Richmond — like staid old Augusta or Charleston — saw itself being transformed into a nightly carnival, and protested. The Richmond *Whig* was speaking for the world of Southern gentility when it called for an end to the "short skirts and *nigger* dancing, ribaldry, blasphemous mock-piety, gross buffoonery and other 'piquant' and profane attractions for the carnal-minded and illiterate."

The South's educational system was shattered by the War. When the young men went off to fight, first as volunteers and later as conscripts, their absence was felt immediately and acutely in the colleges of the South. "I cannot study, and I wish to join a Horse Company," a restless University of Missis-

"Blind Tom" Bethune dazzled audiences during the War with his virtuoso piano performances. Managed by his master, whose surname he adopted, the self-taught slave was endowed with perfect pitch and could reproduce any composition after hearing it only once; he was said to have a repertoire of 7,000 tunes.

sippi student wrote in 1861. He volunteered for service, joined by so many of his classmates that the university closed for the duration. Big and small institutions throughout the Confederacy faced the same problem. At Louisiana's tiny Centenary College the faculty optimistically met for the fall session in October 1861, only to discover that there were no students on campus. "Students have all gone to war," wrote the faculty secretary tersely. "College suspended — and God help the right."

Many of the South's 260 institutions of higher learning closed during the War, including the state universities of Georgia, South Carolina and Louisiana. Although perceptive Southern leaders such as General John C. Breckinridge protested that the Confederacy "cannot afford to 'grind seed corn' in this style," efforts to protect students from conscription failed. Women's colleges were more successful in maintain-

Using this religious pamphle stationery, the Reverend John Jo chaplain of the 8th Geo Regiment, penned a note to his son after the first Confederate vic at Bull Run. Such inspirati pamphlets were widely distrib among the soldiers in the So

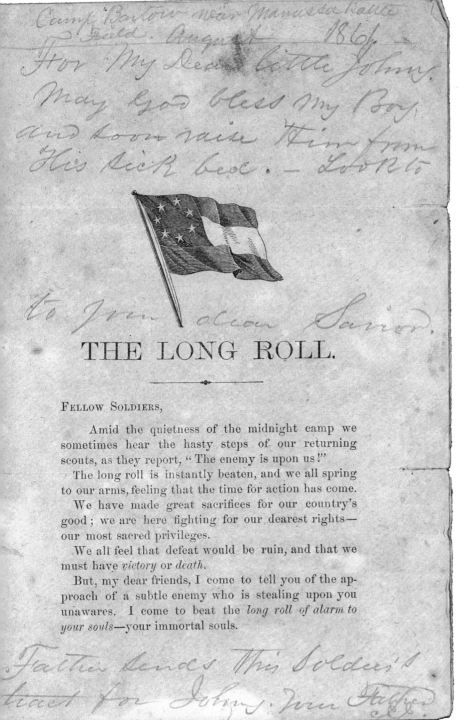

Camp Barlow near Manassa Battle Field. August 1861.

For My Dear little Johny.
May God bless My Boy,
and soon raise Him from
His sick bed. — Look to
to Jesus dear Savior.

THE LONG ROLL.

FELLOW SOLDIERS,

Amid the quietness of the midnight camp we sometimes hear the hasty steps of our returning scouts, as they report, "The enemy is upon us!"

The long roll is instantly beaten, and we all spring to our arms, feeling that the time for action has come.

We have made great sacrifices for our country's good; we are here fighting for our dearest rights—our most sacred privileges.

We all feel that defeat would be ruin, and that we must have *victory* or *death*.

But, my dear friends, I come to tell you of the approach of a subtle enemy who is stealing upon you unawares. I come to beat the *long roll of alarm to your souls*—your immortal souls.

Father sends this soldier's tract for Johny. Your Father

ing their enrollments, but many were shut down by invasion or by the devastating effects of inflation.

Even so, the universities were less endangered by the War than were the public secondary schools — for public education in the South was a recent experiment of uncertain durability. Only North Carolina, Kentucky, Tennessee and Alabama had organized systems of mass public schooling like those common in the North. Other states in the South supported so-called poor schools, established for orphans and children of the impoverished. Schoolteaching was not an esteemed profession, and many positions had been filled by Northerners who either abandoned their posts or were driven out at the onset of war. Still, no one wished to sacrifice the meager beginnings of public education in the South. "Sad, sad indeed will be this war to us," wrote a South Carolina woman to the Charleston *Daily Courier*, "if it results in the utter neglect of our educational interests."

In many rural areas schools simply shut down, leaving "many children growing up in ignorance," as a Virginia woman wrote despairingly to the Governor of her state. Elsewhere, vigorous campaigns were conducted by several educational leaders, of whom the most effective was North Carolina school superintendent Calvin H. Wiley. When he learned that state funds intended for education were being diverted for war purposes, Wiley sent out printed circulars to county officials arguing against the policy, which he termed "suicidal." With the backing of Governor Zebulon B. Vance, Wiley retained enough funds to keep the schools open on a drastically reduced schedule for the remainder of the War.

Near the South Carolina shore, women and children picnic next to a beached "David" torpedo boat, a Confederate navy innovation. The steam-powered

vids — named after the first of their kind — were used in repeated attempts to destroy the Federal vessels blockading Charleston Harbor.

As the pressures on the Confederacy mounted, so did demands for a school curriculum that was biased in favor of the Confederacy. The Athens *Southern Watchman* urged in 1863 that children be taught to detest "not simply the Yankees who are making war on us, but the whole Yankee character." Textbooks supplied by Northern publishers were discarded and new ones written. Johnson's *Elementary Arithmetic,* published in 1864, posed the question, "If one Confederate soldier kills 90 Yankees, how many Yankees can 10 Confederate soldiers kill?" And Mrs. Marinda B. Moore's *Geography* of the same year explained that the principal obstacle to Confederate trade was "an unlawful Blockade by the miserable and hellish Yankee Nation." *The Geographical Reader for Dixie Children,* while conveying the idea that slavery was not sinful and that the slaves were a contented people, also enjoined "all the little boys and girls" to remember "that slaves are human, and God will hold them to account for treating them with justice."

Similar propaganda was drummed into the minds of adults through the agency of Southern churches. A striking aspect of wartime religious expression in the Confederacy was its unanimity: Nearly all faiths and creeds presumed the assistance of God in the conflict and supported the aims of the Confederate government. Such accord was rooted in the conviction that the South was morally superior to the materialistic, mongrel North. Slavery was established by God, and Southerners had been given the responsibility of perpetuating it. Thus the crusade, as Episcopal Bishop Stephen Elliott of Georgia saw it, was to destroy the "infidel and rationalistic principles" of the misguided Yankees—who were attempting to substitute a "gospel of the stars and stripes for the gospel of Jesus Christ."

Sidney Lanier later recalled the extraordinary weight of moral pressure—an "afflatus of war," he termed it—perpetuated by the churches. He compared it to a "great wind," whose "sounds mingled with the solemnity of the church-organs and arose with the earnest words of preachers." As the wind "blew upon all the vanes of all the churches," Lanier remembered, it turned them "one way—toward war."

Failure to support the Confederate cause was, in the eyes of the Methodist Church in the South, sufficient reason for exclusion "from the kingdom of grace and glory." Confederate victories were taken to signify God's "divine presence with us," as one minister put it. Later, as defeats accumulated, churchmen saw God meting out punishment to the South for a whole gamut of transgressions—intemperance, violation of the Sabbath, avarice and lewdness.

The most influential ministers of the war years—men such as the Reverend James Thornwell of South Carolina and the mighty Benjamin Palmer of New Orleans—exhorted Southerners, as Mary Chesnut put it, "to fight and die, a la Joshua." Thornwell spoke of achieving victory "through a baptism of blood." Dr. Robert K. Porter of the Charleston Church of the Holy Communion echoed him by calling upon his congregation to "Fight! fight, my friends, till the streets run blood!"

Some of the militant clergy served in the front lines, and several were cited for gallantry under fire. One chaplain named Brady, in an action near Columbus, Kentucky, shot two Yankees, slashed the throat of another

In an effort to raise money for Confederate Army volunteers, a women's college in North Carolina advertises a benefit concert in this broadside. Southern women staged such fund raisers throughout the War; one statewide drive in South Carolina netted $30,000.

The able administrator of Robertson Hospital in Richmond, Sally Tompkins was the only woman ever commissioned in the Confederate Army. So vital were her services that Jefferson Davis gave her the rank of captain and command of the hospital to ensure her tenure. She accepted on one condition: "I would not allow my name to be placed upon the pay roll of the army."

with a knife and rushed after the retreating enemy crying, "Go to hell, you damned sons of bitches!" The Confederate Chief of Artillery, General William Pendleton, was an ordained clergyman who continued his ministerial duties even in the field—preaching when he was not directing the guns. He was widely quoted in Southern circles as having once said to his men as they eyed the advancing enemy: "While we kill their bodies, may the Lord have mercy on their sinful souls—Fire!"

The fervor of the churches was liberally embraced by the government. In an official pronouncement, Congress gave credit to "the Most High God, the King of Kings and Lord of Lords" for the triumph of Southern arms at Manassas in 1861. Believers claimed that while the battle was being fought, the people of Oglethorpe, Georgia, were praying for the safety of their men—with the result that not a single member of the Oglethorpe Rifles perished, though the unit was in the thick of the fight.

After three years of war and innumerable prayer sessions, President Davis set aside April 8, 1864, as a climactic day of fasting,

humiliation and prayer to invoke divine aid, and to strengthen the resolve of Confederate arms against Grant's impending move on Richmond. In the capital, 5,000 people crowded into the New Richmond Theater to hear the Reverend John L. Burrows call for "the electricity of Heaven" to fall "with destructive violence upon the serried host of the enemy."

The clergy labored so passionately for the Confederate cause that Congressman William Porcher Miles declared "not even bayonets" had done more to sustain the South. But by 1864 morale was slumping and religious ardor growing cold. Membership in the Methodist Church had fallen to scarcely half what it had been in 1860. The Baptists, too, suffered a drastic loss of membership—one large congregation in Georgia shrank to only 11 members.

That same spring, in an effort to buoy the flagging spirits of the people, President Davis sent the respected clergyman George F. Pierce of Georgia on the road to proclaim a new crusade against the heathen Yankees. But by this time the blood-and-thunder clergy had asked too much too often, and few people were inclined to listen. Henceforth the churches directed most of their energies to accelerating a great revivalist wave that swept through the ranks of the Army in the last months of the War. By the autumn of 1864 the Augusta *Baptist Banner* was advising the clergy to visit military encampments to "catch the inspiration of the army in religious things, and carry back to their cold flocks at home some of the fire."

Among other monumental charges, the rigid class structure in the South was permanently transformed. The War engendered contact

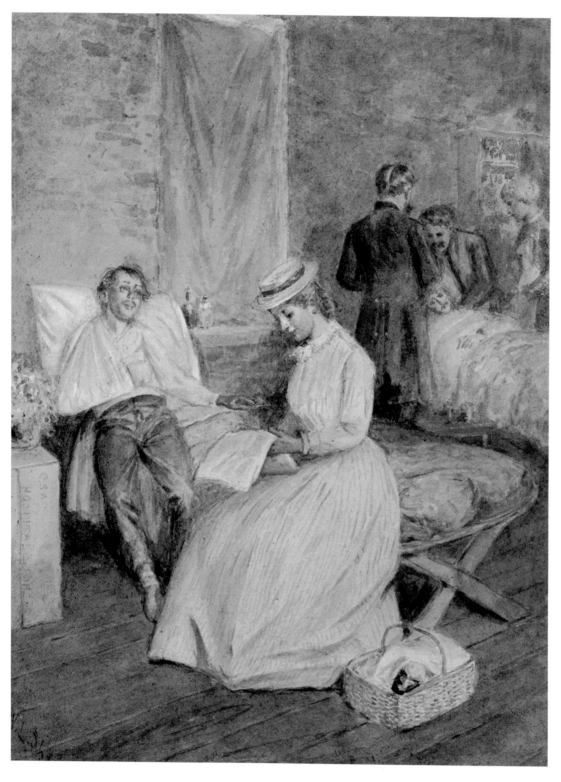

A gaily dressed Southern girl visits a wounded man after the Battle of Bull Run in this 1861 watercolor by soldier-artist William Sheppard. The women were zealous in their compassion for the war victims. When one girl asked a wounded soldier if she might bathe his face, he replied, "Yes, Miss. It's been washed seventeen times already, but go ahead."

between people whose paths would never have crossed in the class-conscious prewar South. Kate Stone, daughter of a wealthy Louisiana planter, noted in her diary with consternation that her brother was compelled to serve as a private in a company whose officers included a livery stable keeper, an overseer and a butcher. The well-born Sarah Morgan was bemused when approached by a Confederate officer whose father, she recalled, sold wares from a cart in the streets of New Orleans. When the officer presumed to speak to her, she judged at once that "the man's respectability was derived from his buttons. That is why he took such pride in them, and contemplated them with such satisfaction. They lent him social backbone enough to converse familiarly with me." Nonetheless, Miss Morgan found herself deeply moved by the "sufferings, privations and heroism" of Confederate prisoners she heard about in detention camps around New Orleans.

Her sense of living in a society whose barriers were crumbling was shared by Mary Chesnut. This genteel young woman, asked to read war bulletins to a group of illiterate Confederate soldiers, was stirred by the simple, serious young men who stood listening, caps in hand.

Women in all classes of Southern society were called on to assume difficult and unfamiliar roles in the absence of able-bodied men. Women became government clerks and factory workers in a society where they had been regarded as fit solely for housekeeping. Plantation mistress Catherine Edmonston discovered that she was as competent as any man to weigh and distribute the allowance of meat for 80 slaves — one half pound of bacon a day for everyone over the age of 10.

Women for the first time replaced male teachers in Southern schools, and assisted male nurses in the crowded hospitals — although notions of female innocence and purity made it impossible for women to attend to the more clinical needs of the wounded. Instead, they might read to wounded soldiers, write letters for them or, on occasion, send notes of condolence to the families of those who died.

Many women of the South who were left to fend for themselves and their families began to question the wisdom of waging a war that was proving so costly in so many ways. They were joined in this inquiry by the poor, the nonslaveholding farmers and others who had precious little to gain from the conflict. In fact, though most Southerners bore up to the War with patience and fortitude, there was far more diversity of opinion and feeling in the South than the Confederate government was willing to acknowledge — or was able to deal with. In time this climate would foster strains of resentment, dissent and even rebellion that would sap the vitality of the Confederate state.

Essentials from Southern Plants

The factory-made, tinned iron canteen *(left)* was preferred by Confederate soldiers to the less durable handmade, wooden canteen *(below)*, bound with hoops. The inscription "Port Hudson" was added by a Federal who claimed the canteen as a trophy of war.

To equip its men for war, the agricultural South was forced to launch new industries for manufacturing a profusion of essential goods and gear.

In Virginia, for example, 120 new enterprises were developed in the first two years of the War. They included textile, flour and paper mills, and a wide variety of cottage industries that turned out crude but serviceable products. In addition, several states set up manufacturing facilities in penitentiaries to enlist convicts in the war effort. One penitentiary in Jackson, Mississippi, housed a cotton mill, a machine shop, and shoe and tailor's shops.

COS

PORT HUDSON

roughly cut cartridge
made of poorly
ed, undyed leather,
produced by a small
hern contractor unused
atherwork.

This carefully crafted
cartridge box, shown open at
right and closed above, was
carried by a Georgia private,
who cut his initials on its
outer flap. It was patterned
after the standard U.S.
Army issue for .58-
caliber ammunition. The
compartmentalized tin insert
held 40 paper cartridges.

black leather belt
w, made by Magee,
er & George of New
ans, has a cap pouch
a brass frame buckle.

Weapons Crafted in Confederate Workshops

This cavalry saber displays a crude finish — particularly when compared with the fine steel products turned out in Northern factories. Its scabbard was made of wood instead of the more lasting but difficult to fashion iron.

Bowie knives of this type were usually made by local blacksmiths to sell to soldiers entering the service. The D-shaped knuckle guard marks the knife as one made for military rather than civilian use.

A fine example of Confederate ordnance, this Enfield-type rifle was manufactured in the factory of Cook & Brother of Athens, Georgia. The Stars and Bars on the lockplate was the company trademark.

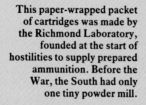

This paper-wrapped packet of cartridges was made by the Richmond Laboratory, founded at the start of hostilities to supply prepared ammunition. Before the War, the South had only one tiny powder mill.

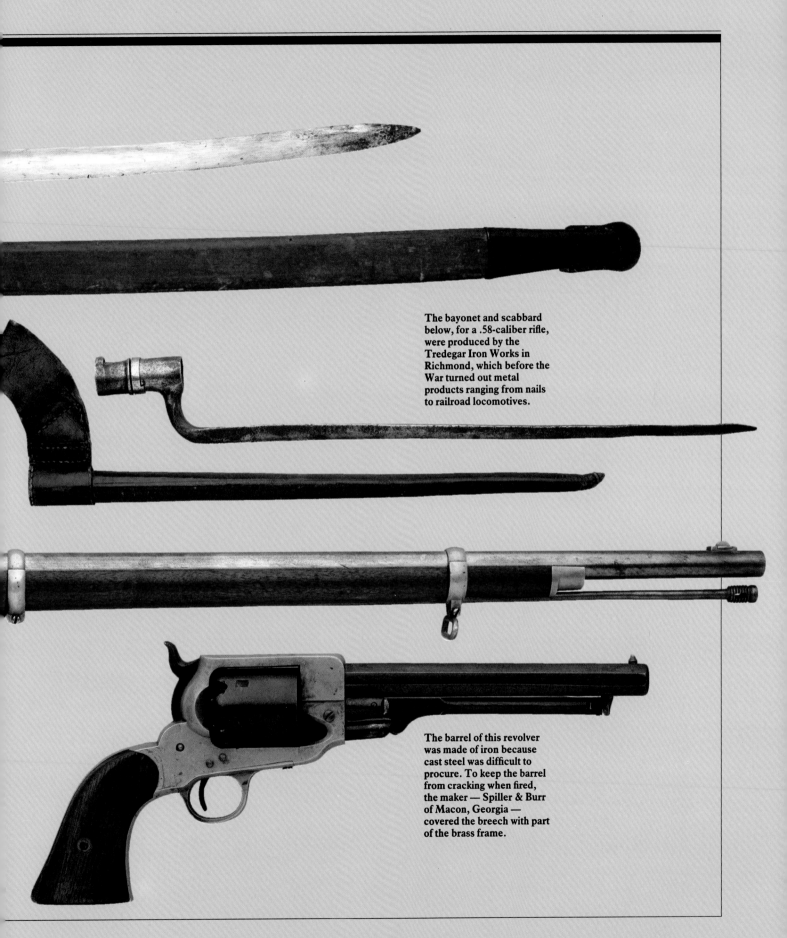

The bayonet and scabbard below, for a .58-caliber rifle, were produced by the Tredegar Iron Works in Richmond, which before the War turned out metal products ranging from nails to railroad locomotives.

The barrel of this revolver was made of iron because cast steel was difficult to procure. To keep the barrel from cracking when fired, the maker — Spiller & Burr of Macon, Georgia — covered the breech with part of the brass frame.

Uniforms Plain and Fancy

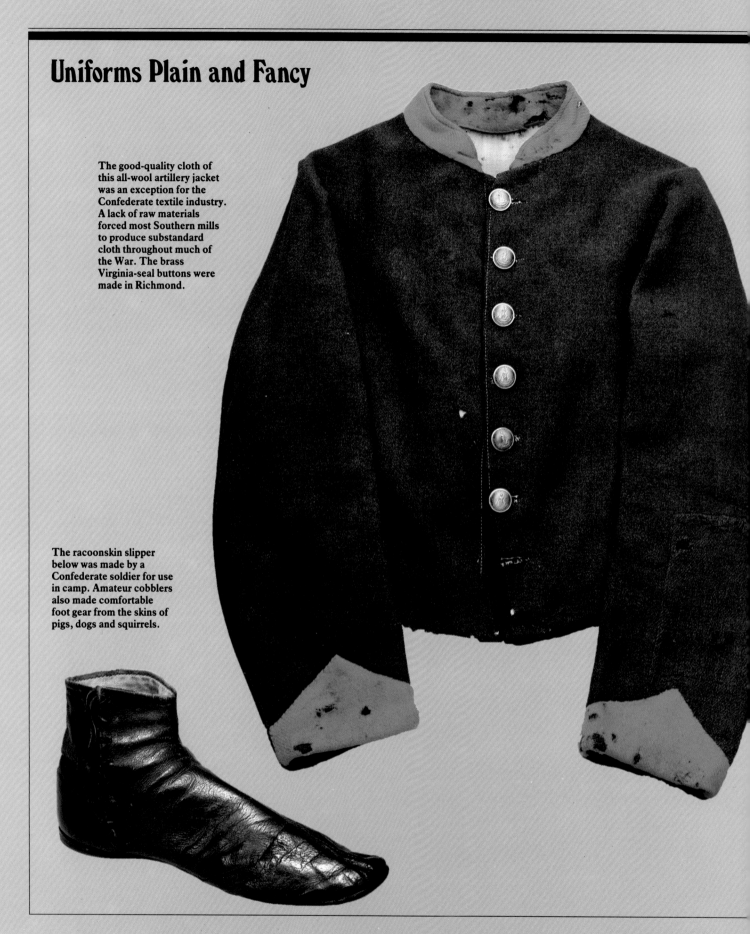

The good-quality cloth of this all-wool artillery jacket was an exception for the Confederate textile industry. A lack of raw materials forced most Southern mills to produce substandard cloth throughout much of the War. The brass Virginia-seal buttons were made in Richmond.

The racoonskin slipper below was made by a Confederate soldier for use in camp. Amateur cobblers also made comfortable foot gear from the skins of pigs, dogs and squirrels.

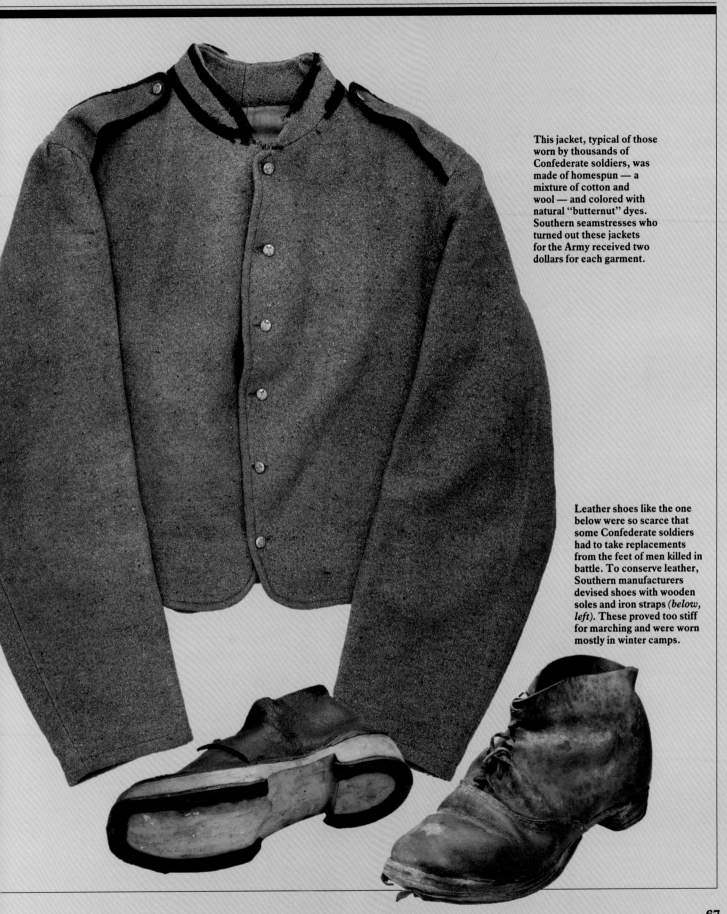

This jacket, typical of those worn by thousands of Confederate soldiers, was made of homespun — a mixture of cotton and wool — and colored with natural "butternut" dyes. Southern seamstresses who turned out these jackets for the Army received two dollars for each garment.

Leather shoes like the one below were so scarce that some Confederate soldiers had to take replacements from the feet of men killed in battle. To conserve leather, Southern manufacturers devised shoes with wooden soles and iron straps (*below, left*). These proved too stiff for marching and were worn mostly in winter camps.

A Cascade of Paper Money

Few nations in history produced such a bewildering variety of paper money as the Confederate States of America. Besides issuing Confederate Treasury notes, the government allowed the circulation of state notes, city notes and notes of private corporations, such as banks and railroads. And as coins became scarce, a few small businessmen in the South created their own paper money to make change for their regular customers.

Lacking printing facilities, the Confederate Treasury at first turned to Northern firms to produce their issues *(below)*. After the outbreak of war, the Treasury was compelled to establish an engraving and lithography plant at Richmond; when that facility could not handle the demand, Treasury officials contracted with a host of small printers. Soon the South was awash with notes of all designs and qualities, some of which are displayed here.

These early-issue Confederate Treasury notes, decorated with pictures of George Washington and the Goddess of Justice, were printed from plates *(opposite)* made by the American Bank Note Company of New York. A branch of the firm operated out of New Orleans under the cover name, the Southern Bank Note Company.

Richmond April 6 1863

Fifty
50
Cents

50
Cents

2ᵈ SERIES

Nº

The Confederate States of America

Will pay **FIFTY CENTS** to bearer.

Tho. Tyler — El Elmore

REGISTER   TREASURER

RICHMOND,   April 6ᵗʰ 1863

1ˢᵗ SERIES

G.   C.

1   1

SIX MONTHS AFTER THE RATIFICATION OF
A TREATY OF PEACE BETWEEN
THE

THE CONFEDERATE STATES & THE
UNITED STATES OF AMERICA.

CONFEDERATE STATES ⸰ AMERICA

Will pay to the bearer on demand

ONE DOLLAR   18047

Nº

M E Norton   W E Dudley

FOR REGISTER.   Engraved by Keatinge & Ball, Columbia S.C.   FOR TREASURER.

RECEIVABLE IN PAYMENT OF ALL DUES EXCEPT EXPORT DUTIES.

SIX MONTHS AFTER THE RATIFICATION   OF A TREATY OF PEACE BETWEEN
THE CONFEDERATE STATES   AND THE UNITED STATES

2   2

FUNDABLE IN EIGHT PER
CENT STOCK OR BONDS OF
THE CONFEDERATE STATES

FIRST SERIES

THE CONFEDERATE STATES OF AMERICA

Will pay **TWO DOLLARS** to Bearer

TWO

Nº   **RICHMOND,**   June 2 1862.

ENG. CAN. COLUMBIA, S.C.

RECEIVABLE IN PAYMENT
OF ALL DUES

The Fires of Dissent

To William Pettigrew and his fellow planters, whose slaves worked the rich land around the North Carolina hamlet of Concord, the day of June 25, 1861, seemed full of hope for the Confederacy.

An outdoor meeting had been called to raise volunteers for the new Confederate Army. Over the excited buzz of the gathering, speakers reviled Lincoln and urged young men to the colors — when suddenly a farmer named Ellsberry Ambrose stepped forward. Ambrose, who owned no slaves but worked his patch of land with his sons, admonished the crowd to ignore the recruiters' harangues. "The rich people," he thundered, "are only going to make the poor people do all the fighting; the rich only pretend to go."

To plantation owners such as William Pettigrew, Ambrose's outburst was tantamount to treason. The infuriated Pettigrew, who held office as a county justice, saw to it that Ambrose was arrested and marched away to jail, where he languished for two months before being released.

But the contentious farmer was soon the center of another storm of controversy. During the next round of recruiting, when the members of a district militia company voted for a man to serve as its captain, the surprise winner turned out to be Ellsberry Ambrose. Outraged by this turn of events, Pettigrew and others warned North Carolina's Governor Henry T. Clark that the newly elected captain might try to march the "true men" of the county right into the hands of the Yan-

kees. Accordingly, the Governor refused to commission Ambrose, and an avowedly loyal Confederate officer temporarily took over the militia company.

Now another of the feisty Ambrose clan, a kinsman named Henry, shouted out his defiance in public: "I am a Lincoln man, and I'll be damned if anyone who voted for Jeff Davis ought not to be hanged."

At that, Pettigrew became truly alarmed and obtained the services of 21 Confederate cavalrymen, who rode into Ambrose territory and hauled the outspoken Henry off to jail. Still, the defiant family was not finished. When a second election was held for militia captain in the area, one Warren Ambrose placed his name on the ballot. Only after he was soundly defeated did the clan declare an uneasy truce in its battle with the Confederacy.

In truth, the problem of deep dissatisfaction over the War was never resolved during the conflict, neither in Concord nor in the rest of the South. It was a bitter fact of the Confederate ordeal that the Southern states, for all the selfless sacrifice of their sons in battle, were riven by dissent and disaffection at home.

Despite the enduring myth of universal commitment to the Confederate crusade, many Southerners — from small farmers to high government officials — detested much of what they were supposed to be fighting for. There never was a solid South living in contented thrall to a plantation society, ready to die for its values. On the contrary, most Southerners held loyalties that were not simply sectional but local — and often intensely personal. The South, in fact, was full of people like Ellsberry Ambrose who cared little for the Confederate design or for its wealthy William Pettigrews; in the dissenters' view, the planters had brought this war upon the common people. And from the outset, such fierce independence and hostility toward authority boded ill for the Confederate cause. "The greatest danger to the new Confederacy," warned the editor of the Augusta, Georgia, *Chronicle* in February of 1861, "arises not from without, not from the North, but from our own people."

The issue of slavery was a particular bone in Southern throats. Some of the most prominent Confederates regarded the institution with abhorrence, as a malignancy eating away at their homeland. President Jefferson Davis himself privately referred to slavery as an "evil," and once told a journalist: "We are not fighting for slavery. We are fighting for independence." Many a plantation owner agreed that if slavery was the cause, it was a bad one. Indeed, slaveholder Ella Clanton Thomas of Georgia felt that slavery "degrades the white man more than the negro," while Tennessee planter Joseph Killibrew confessed that it was a "relic of barbarism." Another planter admitted, "I have often wished to be convinced if in the wrong in owning slaves."

James Madison Wells of Louisiana, holder of 3,000 acres and 96 slaves when the War broke out, needed no convincing. He declared himself against the War — renouncing the role of slaveowner — and holed up in the impenetrable tangles of his hunting preserve, which became a rallying point for other dissidents. At the first good opportunity, Wells made his way onto a Federal gunboat patrolling the Mississippi and thence to occupied New Orleans.

Other well-to-do Southerners took their own roads out. Another Louisiana man, A. P. Dostie, headed for Chicago when asked to sign a Confederate oath; Texan James P. Newcomb left his home for California; Georgia businessman John G. Winter fled all the way to England. And a North Carolina émigré to Indiana reported that "hundreds of Carolinians have arrived in Indiana," adding that nine tenths of the refugees were antislavery as well as pro-Union.

The Southerner's passion for independence spawned a variety of attitudes toward another of the War's driving issues: states' rights. Most people, of course, were quick to affirm the rights of the Confederate states to withdraw from the Union and contest Federal dominance.

The rights of the Confederacy were one thing — but what, exactly, were the rights of an individual Southern state relative to its central government in Richmond? What, moreover, were the rights of the individuals within the Southern states? These were questions that plagued the Confederacy even before the outbreak of war.

When Virginia first voted on its referendum of secession, the 24 northwestern counties stood up for their own rights by declaring 3 to 1 against the proposal, which they viewed as a tidewater planters' idea. In August 1861 they created their own new state of Kanawha — seceding, in effect, from the secession. Kanawha soon renamed itself West Virginia and contributed more than 30,000 soldiers to Federal armies.

The border states of Kentucky and Missouri also refused to break from the Union, though men from both states actually served in the Confederate Congress as so-called ghost representatives of local secessionist constituencies.

Even within the most committed areas of the Confederacy, the matter of the states' proper rights remained problematic — and potentially destructive. A journalist of the time reported that the South had a "not inconsiderable class of men who would draw the sword at the behest of their States as readily against the government of Jefferson Davis as against that of Abraham Lincoln."

Governor Zebulon B. Vance of North Carolina, though strong in his Southern loyalties, expressed them primarily in terms of state supremacy. To Vance the arbiter of North Carolina's fate should remain its people and their state government, not the Confederate government; the commander in chief of North Carolina's militia would continue to be Governor Vance — not any upstart President in Richmond. Among other independent ventures, Vance put together a fleet of state-owned steamers to run the blockade of Federal warships outside Wilmington. The operation proved so successful that one shipment alone provided enough foreign-made uniforms to clothe 14,000 Confederate soldiers.

Georgia's Governor Joseph E. Brown stood out as another feisty defender of states' rights. Brown on one occasion declined to accept a Confederate statute until it had been submitted to the Georgia legislature for ratification. And when Jefferson Davis proclaimed a day of fasting for Confederate victory, Brown ignored it — only to proclaim his own fasting day a week later.

Virginians opposed to secession rally outside the Custom House at Wheeling. There, on June 17, 1861, delegates from the state's northwestern counties voted to disavow the Confederacy and form a Unionist government — a step that led to the creation of West Virginia.

Even so high-ranking a figure as Confederate Vice President Alexander Stephens never hesitated to express disapproval of what was happening in his beloved Southland. "My judgement is against secession," he had remarked at the outset. Stephens stopped short of the sort of protest made by men such as former U.S. Congressman Sherrard Clemens of Virginia, who was sent to prison for publicly swearing allegiance to the Union. But the Vice President was vociferous in his opposition to many of his own government's wartime edicts — conscription, martial law and the suspension of habeas corpus. He regarded them as violations of civil rights and said as much to anybody who would listen.

As the War dragged on, the dissension among the leaders of the Confederacy assumed a shrill, vitriolic tone. And increasingly the invective was aimed in the direction of Jefferson Davis, who as President was a lightning rod for all the South's complaints. Davis did nothing to assuage his many antagonists by maintaining a presidential style that struck them, sometimes with reason, as haughty and unilateral. Congressman Thomas Cobb of Georgia protested that his President "acts for himself and receives no advice except from those who press their advice, unasked."

Mississippian James Alcorn branded Davis a "miserable, arrogant tyrant," and prayed God for Davis to be "damned! and sunk into lowest hell." And one lofty Georgian declined service in the Confederate cause on grounds that "I do not wish my name ever to be enrolled as a 'nigger' of Jeff Davis." The broadest and most profound hatred of Davis seemed to come from Tennessee Congressman Henry Foote, who blasted both the President and his Cabinet: "I hold in contempt him and his whole tribe of servitors and minions."

The incessant clamor of dissent among the rebellion's leaders was the worst possible medicine for the common soldiers and citizens, many of whom neither welcomed nor fully understood the War. The slaughter at Shiloh in the spring of 1862 and the defeat at Antietam that September brought home to the hardscrabble farmers a conviction that they were being impressed for someone else's crusade. They increasingly resisted attempts by the disharmonious planter government to employ them in that crusade, whose principal fruits thus far seemed to be food shortages at home and injury or death on the battlefield.

A back-country North Carolina farm wife, whose husband had gone to soldier, wrote angrily to Governor Vance, "I would like to know what he is fighting for. I don't think he is fighting for anything only for his family to starve." Another North Carolina woman made a more pointed complaint: "The common people is drove off," she wrote, "to fight for the big mans negro."

Thousands of such letters were sent to governors' mansions across the South, supporting Governor Vance's contention that "the great *popular heart* is not now and never has been in the war. It was a case of revolution of the *politicians* and not the *people*." Worse yet, with battlefront casualties on the rise and imports nipped off by the Federal blockade, the politicians were forced to impose a number of measures that the South found unendurable.

The most hated of these measures was conscription. Until the Civil War, no American ever had been drafted by national law into military service. And the South had been especially proud of its army of 12-month volunteers, who had gained the early victories over the Federals. It had been largely an army shaped by the elite. "At the opening of the war," boasted the well-born Southern preacher Augustus B. Longstreet, "our armies were composed mainly of men of wealth, men of the learned professions, students."

The Chatham Artillery of Georgia was a splendid example. As Lieutenant Charles Jones wrote to his father, every new applicant had to be screened and approved by four fifths of the company. As a result, he noted, "We have a company of companions and of gentlemen — men of true courage and men (many of them) with large private interests at stake. I have often thought that if the Chatham Artillery does not render a good account of itself, then one's faith in character, blood and social position may well be shaken." In other such units, a "gentleman private," as South Carolina diarist Mary Chesnut recorded, "took his manservant with him" to clean his boots, polish his sword and forage for rations.

By April of 1862, however, the 12-month enlistments had begun to expire, and a disquieting number of these troops, now battleweary veterans, were heading home to help put in the summer crops — or just plain heading home. To counter this ominous trend, the Confederate Congress resolved to offer a reward of $50 and a 60-day furlough to any man who would reenlist. Officers appealed to the patriotism of their troops, imploring them to stay.

But none of these remedies sufficed, and soon the Richmond *Enquirer* acknowledged

Georgia's independent-minded Governor Joseph E. Brown became thorn in the side of the Confederacy for his fierce defense of local constituents at the expense of the Richmond government. When the Confederate Congress passed a law allowing governors to protect from conscription essential state officers, Brown promptly exempted most of Georgia's civil and military officials.

that the campaign for volunteers was a failure. With casualties climbing at a terrible rate — more than 10,000 at Shiloh alone — the Confederate Congress faced the prospect of waging an ever-expanding war with a shrinking army. Having no other solution, the Congress wrote into law a conscription act, inducting men between the ages of 18 and 35 for three years, if the War lasted that long, and holding the 12-month volunteers for an additional two years.

This measure drew instant fire in the South. Georgian Thomas Cobb, who became a brigadier general in the Army, styled it "an infamous outrage," and many others concurred. Governor Brown blasted the draft for its "unconstitutionality" and then announced: "I cannot permit the enrollment of conscripts under the act of Congress." Governor Vance insisted that he would allow no North Carolina state officials to be taken. And a Confederate soldier in Virginia de-

North Carolina's Governor Zebulon Baird Vance, another avid upholder of states' rights, condemned many actions of the Confederate government, including its appointment of out-of-state officers to command North Carolina troops. "It is mortifying," Vance told his state's legislature, "to find entire brigades of North Carolina soldiers in the field commanded by strangers."

clared that under a law of enforced service, "all patriotism is dead, and the Confederacy will be dead sooner or later."

One of the few positive results of the act was to create a burst of volunteering by men who preferred to sign up for the local militia, hoping for garrison duty around home or, at worst, the chance to march off to war among neighbors rather than strangers. But such recruits usually received only the faintest welcome from their officers. "Although they were not the men upon whom a brave leader would rely for energetic, heroic action," a lieutenant wrote, "they will answer as food for powder and understand how to use a spade." This sort of cynical reception did nothing to sustain the spate of volunteering, and it soon petered out.

There were more appealing alternatives for escaping conscription. The Congress approved a long list of exemptions by which a draftee might avoid service. It was immedi-

ately apparent, however, that these measures favored the wealthy and influential.

One section of the law stated that "persons not liable for duty may be received as substitutes for those who are." This allowed anyone with money to pay a man to serve for him. And 50,000 draftees did so. A lively market developed in which the price of a substitute climbed from $1,600 (plus a fine horse) to $3,000, then to $5,000. One well-to-do landowner from Hanover County, Virginia, offered a 230-acre farm. Newspaper advertisements vied for candidates ($20 a month — offered one ad — and, at war's end, "a fine double-barrelled shot gun"). Alabama's *Clarke County Journal* stated that profits in the tens of thousands had been made by the "most atrocious speculators," some of whom helped sell a man, then connived in his desertion and sold him over and over again. One energetic Richmond substitute, working on his own, peddled himself 20 times.

There were plenty of other ways to dodge the draft, if a man happened to have the right job, or enough influence to secure the right job. The list of legally exempted employments was long, and included mail carrier, telegraph operator, newspaper printer, cotton millworker, apothecary, teacher of more than 20 pupils, minister, railroad hand and, later, munitions worker, tanner, blacksmith, wheelwright and instructor of the deaf, dumb and blind. "Our Bureau of Conscription," commented a clerk at the War Department, "ought to be called the Bureau of Exemptions."

Medical exemptions also proliferated, many of them purchased at exorbitant fees demanded by doctors. Some crooked lawyers charged $500 to engineer either an exemption or a release for a man already in the Army, and freelance counterfeiters sold fake Army discharges for prices that ranged from $400 to $1,000.

All this was occurring at a time when a common soldier's pay was $11 a month in inflated Confederate money. Since the poor lacked the cash to buy their way clear, they surely did become the predominant food for powder. And the conscription laws never offered a single exemption for plain farmers, no matter how many hungry mouths they were forced to leave behind. In the words of one bitterly disaffected Southerner, the Confederate cause was becoming "a rich man's war and a poor man's fight."

Perhaps the most controversial exemption measure of all was the so-called 20-Negro law, which deferred from service any planter or overseer on plantations with more than 20 slaves. The 20-Negro exemption, as a Georgia planter attempted to explain it, would offset "the danger of Negro riots and starvation," by allowing a "few energetic men to remain upon the plantations." The overseers, claimed another supporter, were the "best civil police system that can be invented." If their exemptions were reduced or eliminated, he continued, the "poor white man, the nonslaveholders, would be the greatest sufferers."

Many straight-thinking men in the South believed otherwise. "Never," proclaimed the redoubtable Senator from Mississippi, James Phelan, "did a law meet with more universal odium than the exemption of slave-owners. It has aroused a spirit of rebellion." It also roused the rich to ingenious evasions. The Savannah *Republican* reported that certain plantation owners had divided their slaves into gangs of 20 or more, put them on separate tracts of land, "and made their sons and other relatives overseers to protect them from conscription."

Lacking such alternatives, the poor simply became angrier. "I am informed," said Phelan, that "bodies of men have banded together to resist." In Orange County, Virginia, one John Woolfolk heard farmers "swearing they will be shot before they will fight for a country where the rich men's property is to be taken care of and those who have no overseers are to go and fight first."

Passive resistance to conscription became widespread as thousands of men simply ignored the summons. A contemporary journal reported that in eastern Tennessee "25,500 conscripts were enrolled, and yet only 6000 were added to the army." Confederate Brigadier General Gideon Pillow estimated that 25,000 to 30,000 conscripts in Georgia, where he was stationed, had managed to evade the draft. And Governor John G. Shorter of Alabama admitted, "the enforcement of the act in Alabama is a humbug and a farce."

Altogether, perhaps half of the South's designated conscripts never showed up for duty in the War, a disaster whose consequences fell most immediately upon Robert E. Lee and the men with him at the front. "More than once," said Lee in January 1863, "have most promising opportunities been lost for want of men to take advantage of them, and victory itself has been made to put on the appearance of defeat because our diminished and exhausted troops have been unable to renew a successful struggle against fresh numbers of the enemy."

In an effort to enforce conscription and impose order on the populace, the Confederate Congress permitted generals to declare

A broadside appeals to Tenn[e] men to volunteer before [they are] drafted. After the passage [of the] conscription act of April [1862,] thousands rushed to enlist, no[t] to avert the disgrace of forced se[rvice,] but to ensure their choice of [unit.]

These nattily uniformed mem[bers] of the 2nd Georgia Batta[lion,] shown here with the black slave[s who] served their meals, were am[ong] the many wealthy Southerners [who] formed elite companies i[n the] early months of the War to a[void] serving with their social infe[riors.]

FREEMEN!
AVOID CONSCRIPTION!

The undersigned desires to raise a Company for the Confederate states service, and for that purpose I call upon the people of the Counties of Jefferson and Hawkins, Tenn., to meet promptly at Russellville, on SATURDAY, JULY 19th, 1862, and organize a Company.

By so doing you will avoid being taken as Conscripts, for that Act will now be enforced by order of the War Department. Rally, then, my Countrymen, to your Country's call.

S. M. DENNISON,
Of the Confederate States Army.

CHARLESTON, Tenn., JUNE 30, 1862.

martial law in areas near the front. To make it easier for the government to jail offenders, Davis also persuaded the lawmakers to suspend habeas corpus, the judicial guarantee that a citizen will not be detained illegally. Beginning in 1862, habeas corpus was lifted three different times, for a total of 16 months — all of which only fanned the flames of dissent. Protesting crowds in Richmond grew so threatening on one occasion that the Virginia Senate decided not to convene, and the House adjourned after the opening prayer.

Confederate Congressman Henry Foote compiled what he later called a "shocking catalogue" of questionable arrests following the suspension of habeas corpus. Among the victims was one John M. Higgins of Richmond. The unfortunate Higgins was taken into custody on the ground that one of his distant relatives, a Federal colonel, had written him offering safe conduct through Federal lines to his wife and children should he care to send them North.

Southerners everywhere despised martial law and the military detachments who enforced it. A woman in La Grange, Georgia, told President Davis that the provost guards in her area were nothing but "disgraceful, lawless, unfeeling and impolite men, who were not at the front where patriots and good soldiers are needed. They are running around over town and country insulting even weak unprotected women." When General Braxton Bragg declared martial law around Atlanta, Alexander Stephens remarked that the general had no more right to do so than did "any street-walker in the city."

As part of the wartime restrictions, every citizen traveling through a war zone had to carry a passport — even soldiers on leave.

SUBSTITUTE NOTICES.

WANTED—A SUBSTITUTE for a conscript, to serve during the war. Any good man over the age of 35 years, not a resident of Virginia, or a foreigner, may hear of a good situation by calling at Mr. GEORGE BAGBY'S office, Shockoe Slip, to-day, between the hours of 9 and 11 A. M.   [jy 9—1t*]   A COUNTRYMAN.

WANTED—Two SUBSTITUTES—one for artillery, the other for cavalry service. Also, to sell, a trained, thoroughbred cavalry HORSE. Apply to   DR. BROOCKS, Corner Main and 12th streets, or to   T. T. BROOCKS, jy 9—3t*   Petersburg, Va.

WANTED—Immediately, a SUBSTITUTE. A man over 35 years old, or under 18, can get a good price by making immediate application to Room No. 50, Monument Hotel, or by addressing "J. W.," through Richmond P. O.   jy 9—1t*

WANTED—A SUBSTITUTE, to go into the 24th North Carolina State troops, for which a liberal price will be paid. Apply to me at Dispatch office this evening at 4 o'clock P. M. jy 9—1t*   R. R. MOORE.

WANTED—A SUBSTITUTE, to go in a first-rate Georgia company of infantry, under the heroic Jackson. A gentleman whose health is impaired, will give a fair price for a substitute. Apply immediately at ROOM, No. 13, Post-Office Department, third story, between the hours of 10 and 3 o'clock.   jy 9—6t*

WANTED—Two SUBSTITUTES for the war. A good bonus will be given. None need apply except those exempt from Conscript. Apply to-day at   GEORGE I. HERRING'S, jy 9—1t*   Grocery store, No. 56 Main st.

Advertisements in the Richmond *Dispatch* seek men willing to serve as substitutes for reluctant draftees. The practice of substitution was widely abused: Many men too young, too old or too ill to fight entered the Army as replacements, only to desert within a few days.

Anyone with a missing or questionable passport was held until he could establish satisfactory identity. The system created havoc. Soldiers missed trains waiting for passports to be issued; even the highest officials, in the words of an irate Confederate Congressman, were held up until they could "obtain a pass like a negro." The practice quickly degenerated into farce. "Any villain," reported the Richmond *Whig*, could buy a passport, and "any fool" could forge his own.

The discontent of Southern people was only intensified by growing shortages of food and other necessities — and by new measures the government took to deal with the problem. As time passed, the Federal blockade grew ever tighter, pinching off outside supplies.

Many good farms ceased to produce because their owners had gone to war — or had been disabled or killed on the battlefield.

The Confederate Congress exacerbated the supply situation for civilians in the spring of 1863 by passing a sweeping bill that taxed property, income and profits. The most intrusive of its various measures was a tax in kind on each farm family. The government took 10 per cent of all corn, wheat, rice, cotton, oats, sugar, salt, potatoes, buckwheat, peas, beans, bacon and other meats for the Army. The levy had little effect on a wealthy planter's family. But to a backwoods couple who could barely feed their children and indigent relatives in the best of times, taking away 10 per cent of the food could mean real hardship. To make matters worse, the Confederate Army in 1862 had begun the practice of requisitioning, or "impressing," whatever food and other supplies the gaunt regiments needed as they maneuvered through the countryside.

A resident of Calhoun County, Florida, complained to the Governor of his state, "There are soldiers' families in my neighborhood that the last head of cattle have been taken from them and drove off, and they left to starve."

In North Carolina, Governor Vance reported widespread abuses of the impressment law by poorly disciplined Confederate cavalry, who snatched whatever they fancied despite the pleas of the hapless farmers. And the Richmond *Enquirer* reported, "We often hear persons say, 'The Yankees cannot do us any more harm than our own soldiers have done.'"

Secretary of War James A. Seddon admitted that impressment was "a harsh, unequal, and odious mode of supply." But since in the government's view the alternative to impressment and the tax in kind would be the collapse of the Army, the two despised practices continued. Meanwhile, the Richmond administration was hard-pressed to provide relief programs for the destitute home front. State governments were left mostly to their own devices, and several of them did their best to muster resources to feed and clothe their people.

Georgia's Governor Brown was never one to look elsewhere for help. Unilaterally, he cut taxes for soldiers' families and imposed stays to protect impoverished farmers from having their property seized. He ordered his militia to confiscate the vital raw materials previously impressed by the Army. His legislature allocated money to buy salt — crucial to the preservation of meat — and his militiamen distributed half bushels of it to widows and parents of men killed in action. At one point the state bought 97,500 bushels of corn to pass out to the poor in northern Georgia's devastated red-clay country.

But ultimately, even the most powerful public figures in the South could do little to ease the hardship caused by the War. Nor did they possess the means to stem the tide of corruption that compounded the crisis on the home front. As shortages worsened, hoarding escalated and price gouging by shopkeepers became common. Greater profit resulted from more imaginative ventures, however. Planter James Alcorn of Mississippi spent the entire War admittedly "hiding and selling" his cotton to the Union and the Confederacy impartially. He wrote his wife that on one occasion in the late fall of 1862 he had sold 111 bales at 40 cents a pound to Northern agents, with 90 more ready to ship. After his wife implored him to stop he replied, "I wish to fill my pockets. I can in five years make a larger fortune than ever." Nor was Alcorn by any means alone: "It is obvious," recorded one diarist, "that the cotton sold by Mr. Dunnock in the enemy's country will be very *comfortable* to the enemy. And it may aid Mr. Dunnock in accumulating a fortune."

Another type of graft was practiced by so-called commissary vultures, who used their employment in Army depots as a license to steal. These men received the food and other goods seized from the people and brought into the depots — but never passed it on to the troops. Instead, they sold the goods surreptitiously at prices beyond the reach of all but the wealthy.

Partly as a result of such corruption, the average family food bill, in the estimation of the Richmond *Dispatch*, climbed from about $6.65 per month at the time of secession to $68 by early 1863. Common soap had increased in price from 10 cents a pound to $1.10 — one tenth a soldier's monthly pay — and half a pound of green tea now cost $16. "So much we owe the speculators," the *Dispatch* observed, "who have stayed at home to prey upon the necessities."

A tax assessment form notifies an Alabama hog farmer that he owes the Confederate government one tenth of the pork from his slaughtered hogs, payable in bacon. Farmers resented giving the government such valuable products; they would have preferred to pay their taxes in the inflated Confederate currency.

A white overseer and two slaves guard their master's cotton in a Mississippi swamp until the crop can be sold to Northern agents. But only a few Southern planters managed to smuggle their cotton into Northern markets; Confederate soldiers saw to it that most Southerners burned the staple to prevent it from falling into Federal hands.

Tolerance for such speculators among the people eventually expired, and nasty incidents occurred in a dozen places around the South in the spring in 1863. In Atlanta a pistol-carrying woman led a group of citizens into a butcher shop and asked the price of bacon. When advised that it was $1.10 per pound, the leader showed the gun, telling her companions to take all they wanted. She then led them into other shops; they quickly persuaded a number of storekeepers to sell at lower prices, but the stubborn ones among the owners were told simply to hand over the goods.

On April 2, 1863, in Richmond, a group of angry women met at a Baptist church on Oregon Hill under the leadership of one Mary Jackson, described in a contemporary account as a "tall, daring, Amazonian-looking woman with a white feather erect from her hat" and a "six-shooter" in her hand. In a rousing speech, Mrs. Jackson told the women they should demand food at fair prices or take it by force. Her listeners poured out onto the streets, their numbers swelling to several hundred, men among them, as they marched to Capitol Square. There the crowd halted while Mary Jackson and others pre-

sented their grievances to Governor John Letcher. The Governor listened sympathetically, but when he failed to make concessions, the mood of the group turned violent. Shouting and brandishing knives and hatchets, the mob surged into the city's shopping district. The women smashed windows and rampaged into stores, wrecking the interiors, taking clothing along with food. The crowd even invaded a hospital and looted 300 pounds of beef from the commissary.

A company of soldiers arrived and began pushing the mob up Main Street. As the people glared at the soldiers and the situation seemed certain to end in bloodshed, President Jefferson Davis himself appeared on the scene. Davis climbed atop a wagon and called on the mob to disperse. The rioters hissed and booed in reply, and surged restlessly around Davis' wagon. "You say you are hungry and have no money — here is all I have," Davis cried out, shoving his hands into his trousers. "It is not much, but take it," he said, slinging the contents of his pockets into the crowd. Then from his vest Davis removed his watch and held it up for all to see. "We do not desire to injure anyone, but this lawlessness must stop. I will give you five minutes to disperse. Otherwise you will be fired upon."

The crowd grew silent. The soldiers prepared arms while Davis continued to look at his watch, then at the unhappy gathering around him. At last, by ones and twos and then by dozens, the crowd left the square, melting into the side streets of Richmond. The bread riot was over.

By the autumn of 1863 the civil deprivations and military defeats had combined to produce profound discouragement among the people of the South. They bent under the deadening weight of a war that no longer seemed to promise victory. The fact was, as General Kirby Smith reported to President Davis, "the common folk were tired of fighting; they simply wanted the boys to come home." This sentiment had already extended to the Army, where it was doing mortal harm to the Confederate cause. Thousands of the boys already were coming home — without leave. At the end of 1863 the roster of the entire Confederate Army numbered 465,000 men. In fact, only 278,000 men remained on duty; fully 187,000 were absent, with or without leave. And there seemed little chance of getting most of them back.

Robert E. Lee said he believed that "insufficiency of food and non-payment of the troops had more to do with dissatisfaction among the troops than anything else." Some regiments, through confusion or plain lack of funds, had received no pay for six to 10 months. In Tennessee, General James Longstreet's men got only half rations of meat and bread — and counted themselves lucky. An artillery battalion on the march lived for a week mainly on the corn issued for their horses, and two deserters said their cavalry company had gone for two days on wild berries and persimmons.

Still, some Confederate authorities believed that the soldiers were less discouraged by their own condition than by the plight of those at home. And in truth, the pleading letters that poured into Army camps from wives and other family members were the ultimate cause of many desertions.

The authorities tried to discourage such pessimistic messages from home. An Alabama official counseled in a newspaper:

Virginia politician John Minor B... shown here seated with his fa... spent eight weeks in a Richmon... for openly challenging the legali... the Confederacy. But most other Union Virginians kept silent. W... Botts: "All were afraid to exp... their opinions, under the rei... terror and demands of despotism... had been established in Richmo...

"Wives! Mothers! beware what you write. A thoughtless and imprudent letter may lead to discontent, desertion."

But the people at home could scarcely contain their misery. "Our son is lying at death's door," a despairing wife wrote to her soldier husband. "He is raving distracted, his earnest calls for Pa almost breaks my heart. John come if you can."

A soldier in the 64th North Carolina Volunteers received this letter: "The people is all turning Union here since the Yankees has got Vicksburg. I want you to come home as soon as you can. The conscripts is all at home yet." A deserter by the name of Edward Cooper, when caught and put on trial for his life, produced in his defense a letter in which his wife pleaded, "before God, Edward, unless you come home we must die." When the court nevertheless condemned Cooper to death, Robert E. Lee personally pardoned him.

Whether from mercy or plain practicality — the Confederacy could hardly hang or shoot 100,000 soldiers, and besides, a pardoned man might rejoin the Army — a general policy of forgiveness toward deserters prevailed from midwar onward. In August 1863, Davis proclaimed an amnesty for any deserter who came back within 20 days. Shortly thereafter, the Confederate Congress offered $100 bonds to soldiers who promised not to desert. Virginia's General John Clifford Pemberton made a virtue of necessity by declaring a 30-day leave for his men, "as they had all gone to their homes without leave."

But some officials showed little mercy, trying to stop the runaways by threat and punishment. A few commanders branded captured deserters with a C for "coward," or meted out 39 lashes — or issued the death penalty. A soldier from North Carolina saw three men executed and reported home, "I heard that they were caused to desert by letters from home."

Not surprisingly, the business of finding deserters and bringing them back became an increasingly high-risk occupation. Two

en to desperation by food
rtages and impossibly high prices,
gry women ransack a bakery in
mond on April 2, 1863, a day of
espread looting in the capital city.

North Carolina officers who tried to stop a group of deserters were shot to death for their trouble, and when the authorities finally caught the killers, the state's Chief Justice released them on a writ, saying the slain officers had exceeded their authority. In Alabama, a local judge was so frightened of disgruntled deserters that he refused to convene his court at all without a military guard to protect him.

Though a great many men who deserted came home seeking little more than peace with their families, others returned spoiling for trouble. As their numbers increased, these fugitives tended to band together for protection against the authorities. In order to sustain their enclaves, they inevitably resorted to plunder. And when threatened with capture, they reacted with violence.

In North Carolina, Governor Vance was told by an officer that fugitives "now bring with them Government arms and ammunition, and officers are sometimes shot by them and the community kept in terror." In South Carolina, deserters built a log fort as a makeshift headquarters, from which they rampaged through the countryside, burning courthouses and bridges, and herding off hogs and cattle by the score. A deposition against them stated that they would "hang a man by the neck till he is almost lifeless to make him tell where his money and valuables are."

In time the fugitive bands expanded, amassing the strength and firepower to control large amounts of territory. Most often they established their fiefdoms in the hills and crags of the Appalachians, terrain that offered natural protection against the authorities. The paths leading into these strongholds tended to be narrow and rocky,

difficult for cavalrymen to negotiate in the friendliest of times. Now any intruders could be watched by sentinels who signaled the approaching danger by cowbells, hunting horns or the whoop of a hog call. A quilt hung on a cabin yard fence in a particular position might warn a fugitive husband that government men were nosing around. The authorities trespassed those alien grounds at great risk — knowing full well that deserters often shot officers on sight. In mountainous Floyd County, Virginia, the sizable Sisson clan set up a so-called deserter kingdom, ruled by fugitives in the family, who welcomed other trustworthy runaways.

A deserter fiefdom in the hills of South Carolina reportedly sprawled over a 40-by-60-mile area. In this vast domain, conceded a Confederate officer, "almost every pass and valley is occupied by a deserter's cabin, who on the approach of a stranger flies to the rocks and ravines where, taking his perch, he sees and observes all that is going on, safe from the eye of his pursuer."

Few of those who lived near the deserters' citadels were willing to aid the authorities. Many families had relatives among the fugitives; other people had been drained of all loyalties by the deprivations they had suffered and wanted nothing more than to mind their own business. When Confederate officers in South Carolina asked for help in ferreting out the leaders of one fugitive band, they found only antipathy. "The people there," wrote one officer, "are poor, ill-informed, and but little identified with our struggle. They have been easily seduced from their duty."

In other places, fugitive bands made a conscious effort to gain the support of the populace. A Mississippi gang assured itself

89

Confederate Vice President
Alexander Hamilton Stephens
undercut the authority of President
Jefferson Davis at every opportunity,
citing an obligation to defend
the liberties guaranteed by the
Confederate Constitution. "Away
with the idea of getting independence
first and looking after liberty
afterward," he warned. "Our liberties,
once lost, may be lost forever."

of local support by helping shorthanded families with their farm work. Squads of 40 or 50 deserters, hauling threshers and other machines, would arrive at a farm, post pickets and set to work. If the farmer was inclined to make whiskey, so much the better. By one account bands of fugitives "congregated at stillyards, where they distilled quantities of liquor, cut and rolled logs and repaired fences, and swore vengeance against anyone who approached with the intention of molesting them."

The bitterness and antagonism toward authority that smoldered in the hearts of many of the fugitives sometimes ignited, turning the mountains into small-scale battlegrounds. In the hills of Madison County, North Carolina, on a cold January night in 1863, about 50 men, mainly deserters from the local 64th North Carolina, slipped into the hamlet of Marshall to raid for salt stored there by their old regiment. In the course of the foray they wounded a captain who was home on leave, and broke into the house of a thoroughly disliked colonel named Lawrence Allen.

At the time of the attack, Allen was away at the regiment's camp in Bristol, Tennessee, 60 miles northeast of Marshall. But his wife and children — two of the youngsters deathly ill with scarlet fever — were at home. They stood by terrified as the fugitives smashed Allen's trunks and snatched money and clothes before vanishing into the snowy darkness toward their hide-outs in the nearby Laurel Valley.

When word of the raid reached Bristol, Allen and another officer, James Keith, got permission from General Henry Heth, the regional commander, to punish the raiders. "I want no reports from you about your course at Laurel," Heth is supposed to have said. "I do not want to be troubled with any prisoners and the last one of them should be killed." Meanwhile, loyal troops from Marshall had pursued and overtaken the raiders, killing 12 and capturing 20.

Then two columns of the 64th under Allen and Keith moved into the Laurel Valley separately, plowing through hip-deep snow and enduring a bitter wind. Slogging into a tiny settlement, Allen's men heard the blaring of hunting horns. Rifles crackled from behind trees and rocks; Allen's troops returned the fire, and soon 14 of the raiders lay dead and others were in flight. That night Allen got the news that his son had died of the fever and his daughter was on the verge of death.

Two days later Allen and his wife buried their two children. The next morning Allen joined forces with Keith on a vengeance sweep through the valley. They burned barns and killed livestock. Finding no men in the houses, they commenced to torture women and children. Eighty-five-year-old Unus Riddle was strung up, whipped and robbed. Seventy-year-old Sally Moore was whipped until she bled. And another woman was tied to a tree in the snow, with her infant exposed to the freezing cold at an open cabin door, until she told where the men were hiding. Finally she — or someone else — talked, permitting Keith to round up 15 male prisoners, of whom two quickly escaped.

Learning of the situation in the Laurel Valley, Governor Vance dispatched a telegram to General Heth: "Do not let our excited people deal too harshly with these misguided men. Please have them delivered to the proper authorities for trial." At the scene, the remaining prisoners were assured that they would get a fair hearing.

A detachment under Keith started down the main road that led out of the valley. Suddenly, at a clearing, the soldiers halted the prisoners. Five were ordered to kneel down, while a file of soldiers lined up 10 paces away. An old man named Joe Woods cried, "For God's sake, men, you are not going to shoot us?"

Keith ordered his soldiers to fire. They hesitated. He commanded, "Fire or you will take their place." A ragged volley cracked, and four of the prisoners fell dead; a fifth, wounded in the stomach, pleaded for mercy but got a bullet in the head. A few moments later, five more prisoners, and then another three, knelt to take the volleys. This time a 13-year-old boy named David Shelton did not quite die. He crawled toward the fir-

ing squad, begging, "You have killed my old father and three brothers. Let me go home to my mother and sisters." A final bullet silenced him.

The soldiers shoved the heap of bodies into a shallow hole hacked from the icy ground and covered them with loose dirt. When their families came upon the dead the next day, wild hogs had begun to feed on the corpses.

Not long after this murderous episode, far to the south in the pine woods of eastern Mississippi, there erupted a rebellion that demonstrated how deep the vein of dissension ran in the Confederacy.

It began when Newton Knight, a shoemaker in Jones County, was conscripted into the Army. A Unionist at heart, Knight re-

Concealed amid boulders in the east Tennessee mountains, pro-Union guerrillas ambush Confederate cavalry trying to track down Army deserters. Union sentiment ran so high in the region that deserters, when captured, often fled again at the earliest opportunity. "I know many deserters now in desertion for the fourth, fifth and sixth times," a judge complained to President Davis.

fused to fight and was allowed to serve locally as a hospital orderly with the 7th Mississippi. But Knight remained discontent, and when Confederates confiscated his mother's horse, he abandoned his regiment and headed for the woods and swamps.

There he was joined by Jaspar Collins, another deserter who was outraged by the 20-Negro exemption for wealthy planters. By mid-1863, the two had recruited about 80 other unyielding dissenters and had vowed "to form a home defense band for resistance to oppression, by assassination, raiding, destruction, and other means to aid the Union, and at the same time to save our families from famine."

Led by Knight, who carried a double-barrelled 12-gauge shotgun dubbed "Sal" and signaled his band with an elegant ebony hunting horn, the dissenters lived up to their charter. They quickly won popular sympathy by their concern for the poor, particularly local families whose Unionist loyalties had earned them harsh treatment from conscription, tax and impressment agents. On one raid into a neighboring county, Knight's marauders came back with six wagonloads of corn, which they shared with destitute families. In return, farm wives often smuggled food to Knight's band, and on one occasion an especially grateful woman somehow managed to furnish Knight with 50 pounds of lead for shot.

The guerrillas made their headquarters in a cave they called "the Devil's Den," situated on an island in the Leaf River. From this refuge they sallied forth to sink ferryboats, burn bridges and bushwhack Confederates along the roads. They ran one tax-in-kind collector out of Jones County, and when two others tried to resume the collections, Knight's men shot them dead.

By 1864 the renown of the fugitives was such that a young Confederate officer reported they "held supreme control over Jones County and the surrounding Counties." He added that they had established a "Republic of Jones" right there in Mississippi, "complete with President, Vice-President, Cabinet and an army of several hundred men."

Actually, Knight and Collins claimed no titles and never commanded more than 125 men. But tales of their exploits circulated until the gang's fief entered legend as the "Free State of Jones." And free its soldiers remained, working their will in deadly fashion. Although Confederate soldiers were the primary targets, the gang readily shot any citizen who refused to hand over supplies. Killing in Jones County became such a commonplace occurrence, a citizen named B. C. Duckworth complained, that "if a man is found dead the civil authorities pays no attention to it — any more than if it was a dog."

When cavalry detachments tried to catch Knight's men, the fugitives either ambushed the horsemen or melted into the swamps. Efforts to persuade their women to talk were useless. One wife, questioned by cavalrymen about her husband, responded, "I told you the truth; I don't know where he is, but I can find out." Picking up a hunting horn, she blew three sharp notes. When the encircling woods reechoed a chorus of answering calls, the alarmed troopers, thinking themselves surrounded, fled at a gallop.

A decree of amnesty from General Leonidas Polk failed to bring in Knight or his men. Quite the contrary. Word came from the back country that the Jones County irregulars were ready to raid repair crews

working on Mobile & Ohio railway bridges in the area. That was too much for the commander of the Army's Department of the Gulf. In March 1864, he dispatched Colonel Henry Maury with a sharpshooter battalion, a detachment of horse artillery and 200 cavalrymen to break up the gang. "This wasn't going to be easy," recalled a captain assigned to the force, "and we were troubled over the prospect."

His concern was borne out by the fierce antagonism exhibited by the first prisoners. One man, captured with his brother, was offered freedom if he would join the Confederates. He replied: "Hell, no, I'll shoot you every one. I'll shoot every chance I get as long as I live." The brothers were quickly hanged. So were four other men captured after a fight in which they killed or wounded several Confederate soldiers. Nine more fugitives swiftly met death as Colonel Maury pressed the chase.

One man, a Confederate deserter, was shot in full view of his wife and new baby when he tried to slip into an Army-occupied area to visit them. Then, in a dreadful error, the soldiers arrested Newton Knight's cousin Ben, an officer home on leave from the Confederate Army. Believing that they had at last captured the gang's leader, they strung him up on the spot, and displayed the body to Newton's wife. In revulsion and horror, she pointed out their mistake—confirmed by leave papers discovered on

the dead man. Newton Knight more than evened the score. On the 26th of April, he and his men ambushed a cavalry patrol and killed 15 soldiers.

Nevertheless, by late spring the Confederate troops claimed to have wiped out all of the guerrillas save Knight and about 20 of his cohorts. A pack of 44 bloodhounds was brought in to run the fugitives to ground. But it was the dogs that ran down, some of them poisoned by the locals; shortly only two hounds remained. At last, that Christmas, at a wedding by the Leaf River in a place called Cracker's Neck, 100 cavalrymen jumped the celebrating men and wounded and almost captured Knight; still, he managed to lead most of his guerrillas back to safety deep in the swamps, where he recovered from his wounds.

Thus Newton Knight survived the War. He was never tried or punished. He had fought against people and policies that intruded upon his small corner of the world and threatened his independence. So, too, in some degree, had thousands of other Southern men and women, by registering their protests against wartime policies that proved grossly inequitable and, finally, intolerable. From the highest reaches of the government to its lowest hardscrabble farms, the Confederacy was a nation divided. More than the lack of rifles, perhaps, it was the lack of unity among the Confederacy's people that crippled its bold move toward nationhood.

Diarist Sarah Morgan

A Chronicler of the Occupation

"The excitement has reached the point of delirium — we only know we had best be prepared for anything," wrote 20-year-old Sarah Morgan when she heard about the fall of New Orleans in April 1862. The news fed her worst fear — that the Yankees would come up the Mississippi River and conquer her hometown of Baton Rouge, Louisiana's peaceful state capital. Indeed, scarcely a month later, the first Federal gunboats arrived, and for the next three years, this wellborn young woman set down in a diary her account of life under enemy rule.

The War had divided Sarah's family. A brother living in New Orleans had declared for the Union. Three others were off fighting for the Confederacy. Sarah, her two sisters and widowed mother were left to fend for themselves in Baton Rouge. Pretty and impressionable, Sarah at first found some of the Federal officers as gallant as any Southern gentleman. But as the realities of war came to Baton Rouge, she lost her romantic notions.

In this wartime photograph of Baton Rouge, shops line Laurel Street as it approaches Church Street, where Sarah Morgan lived.

First Impressions of a Powerful Foe

"About sunset, a graceful young Federal stepped ashore, carrying a Yankee flag, and asked the way to the Mayor's office." Thus did Sarah Morgan describe the capture of Baton Rouge. At first, such polite formalities prevailed. "These people," she confided to her diary, "have disarmed me by their kindness. I admire foes who show so much consideration for our feelings."

Sarah and her sisters received soldiers in their home and took girlish delight in watching the troops drill. "One conceited, red-haired lieutenant smiled at us in the most fascinating way," she gushed. "Perhaps he smiled to think how fine he was, and what an impression he was making." But when a Federal officer offered to place a guard around the Morgan home to protect it against vandals, Sarah advised her mother that acceptance would smack of collaboration. And she worried lest she become too familiar. "Why wasn't I born old and ugly?" she lamented. "Suppose I should unconsciously entrap some magnificent Yankee! What an awful thing it would be!"

Federal soldiers from the troopship
Sallie Robinson form ranks on Main
Street. The troops, wrote Sarah, were
"stared at unmercifully and pursued
by crowds of ragged little boys."

The camps of two of the regiments occupying Baton Rouge — the 7th Vermont and the 21st Indiana — sprawl across an expanse of open land on the east side of t

A family and their slaves comb through the ruins of their burned-out home in August 1862, after the Federals reduced a third of Baton Rouge to rubble.

Before it was gutted by fire, the Louisiana State House was used by the Federals to hold prisoners.

The Ruin of a Town

The honeymoon between the occupiers of Baton Rouge and the townsfolk ended abruptly in late May of 1862 when Confederate guerrillas wounded three Federal sailors. Federal gunboats retaliated by shelling the city. Then, on August 5, a 2,600-man Confederate force attempted to retake the city and was repulsed only after a bloody fight in which each side suffered 84 killed.

Fearing a second attack, the Federals chopped down many magnificent shade trees to furnish wood for abatis. And to provide a clear field of fire around Federal defense lines, houses and buildings were put to the torch.

Sarah Morgan, who had taken refuge on a relative's plantation, returned to find Baton Rouge "hardly recognizable."

Three Union officers chat with a civilian visitor outside their tent. The chairs and wooden tent flooring were stolen from Baton Rouge homes.

Collapse of Civility

After the Confederate attempt to regain the city, many Federals dropped all pretense of civility and began wholesale looting. "Ours was the most shockingly treated house in the whole town," Sarah wrote. The Federals stole china, carpets and clothing, slashed family portraits, and smashed furniture that was too big to be carted off.

Sarah was particularly mortified to find that the looters had rummaged through her keepsakes, including dried roses and letters from gentlemen friends. "As I looked for each well-known article," she commented bitterly, "I could hardly believe that Abraham Lincoln's officers had really come so low down."

Sheltered by tents from the blazing sun, Federal officers and their wives enjoy an outing beside the Mississippi.

A battery of Massachusetts field artillery stand in formation in front of a barracks in Baton Rouge prior to the attack on Port Hudson.

A crowd of teamsters, some of them blacks who stayed in Baton Rouge after their masters fled, awaits the unloading of the wharfboat *Natchez* in the spring of 1863.

"At the Mercy of the Yankees"

In early 1863, Baton Rouge became a staging area for the Federal assault on nearby Port Hudson, and the number of troops in town swelled to a wartime high of 17,000. Meanwhile, along with most of the white population, the Morgans had sought refuge in the Confederate-held countryside.

"It has come at last," wrote Sarah, listening to the distant Federal bombardment of Port Hudson at 1:30 a.m. on March 15. "What an awful sound. Baton Rouge was child's play compared to this."

The Port Hudson defenses held. But food supplies for the refugees were dwindling. "Not a scrap of meat in the house for a week," Sarah wrote. "What can we do? The whole country is at the mercy of the Yankees. Mother is not in a condition to stand such privation."

A wooden signal tower overlooks a Federal cavalry camp at the north end of Baton Rouge.

The Louisiana Institute for the Deaf, Dumb and Blind, the largest building in Baton Rouge, became a Federal hospital during the battle for Port Hudson.

A Tide of Disease and Death

As the siege of Port Hudson dragged on, ships steamed downriver from the battlefield laden with casualties. In Baton Rouge, private homes, barracks, the hotel and other buildings were converted into hospitals. But in many cases, the makeshift infirmaries proved little more than death wards as thousands of the wounded succumbed to infection and disease.

With no possibility of returning home, the Morgans fled to New Orleans and the care of Sarah's older brother. To enter the city, Sarah had to "turn Yankee" by swearing allegiance to the United States. But a worse ordeal awaited her. In March 1864 word came that two of her brothers in the Confederate forces had died of disease. "O God, O God, have mercy on us!" Sarah wrote. Thereafter, her diary entries were fewer and more terse. And never again did she return to her beloved Baton Rouge.

Graves of young soldiers, members of the 52nd Massachusetts, lie in a Baton Rouge cemetery. The men died of disease, not in action.

Long Cruel Roads

"We cannot look into the future of this world at all. We cannot form an idea as to where or in what condition we may be one month hence."

BETTY HERNDON MAURY, REFUGEE IN VIRGINIA

When General Robert E. Lee arrived at Richmond in April 1861 to take command of Virginia's military forces, he wrote home to his wife, Mary Custis, at their estate across the Potomac from Washington, warning her that she was in danger of being captured by Federal troops. He implored her to pack and leave as soon as possible.

At first she resisted, but she could hear the sounds of drumbeats and cannon fire drifting menacingly from the far side of the river. Finally, Mary Custis Lee took what possessions she could and fled. "All Virginia has open doors for the family of General Lee," wrote a neighbor, and indeed, Mrs. Lee had need of such hospitality. In her fifties, crippled by arthritis, she spent the remainder of the War traveling from one relative or friend to another, destined never to return home.

Mrs. Lee was but one victim in a mass displacement of Southerners — refugees who crowded the roads, trains, towns and cities of the region in a futile search for sanctuary from the Federal invaders. Thousands upon thousands of whites fled from the occupying armies of the North. At the same time, even larger numbers of slaves were uprooted with their refugee owners, or fled by themselves to freedom within Federal lines.

The civilians of the Union suffered nothing like these agonies of invasion and displacement. Few Northerners faced soldiers at their own front doors. Few saw their homes burned, their food confiscated, their livestock and wagons driven off. Thus when a Virginia woman named Judith McGuire heard rumors of an impending battle in Pennsylvania, she wrote: "So may it be! We are harassed to death with their ruinous raids, and why should not the North feel it in its homes? Nothing but their personal suffering will shorten the war. I want their horses taken for our cavalry and wagons, in return for the hundreds of thousands that they have taken from us; I want their fat cattle driven into Virginia to feed our army."

In the South, such pillage and suffering was commonplace. Fighting a war that was primarily defensive, the rebellious states had to deal with an aggressor on their own territory. And each wave of enemy penetration, as it smashed through farmlands and cities in Virginia, Louisiana, Mississippi, Tennessee, Georgia and finally the Carolinas, compelled thousands to choose between flight or life under the conquerors.

The choice was an easy one only for Union sympathizers, who welcomed the Federal troops. For everyone else, the decision could be agonizingly difficult. The most compelling reason to remain at home was to protect one's property — in whatever way possible. "It is evident," reasoned one plantation matron in deciding to remain, "if my dwelling is left unoccupied everything will be sacrificed." Indeed, some Federal generals sent proclamations ahead of their advance columns, urging owners of businesses, farms and plantations to remain at home as the

Mrs. S. D. Drewry of Chesterfield County, Virginia, strikes a defiant pose with a riding crop she used to drive off a Federal officer who tried to enter her house. "The women were, by all odds, far worse rebels than the men," wrote an observer who accompanied General George B. McClellan on the 1862 Peninsular Campaign in Virginia.

best safeguard against looting or vandalism.

One spunky Southern girl, Cordelia Lewis Scales, related in a letter to a friend how she stayed at home as urged and stood up to a Federal detachment that camped on her family's land. A young lieutenant spoke to her: "He wanted to know what I styled them," she wrote. "I told him Yankees or Negro thieves, and if they whipped this part of our army that we had girls and boys enough to whip them. He then told me that such bravery should be rewarded — that nothing on the place should be touched. He made all the men march before him and he did not let them trouble anything."

The pluck of this young woman — and others like her — proved out the policy. For as the invaders struck deeper, the places most severely pillaged were those abandoned by their owners. Despite orders to the troops from some commanders to respect private property, a house standing empty, an open pantry or liquor closet, or a lone horse presented irresistible temptation to soldiers on the move. Later in the War, when General William Tecumseh Sherman and others told their far-flung invaders to live off the land, the presence of an owner did not prevent Federal soldiers from taking whatever they needed. But it usually kept them from stealing or destroying everything.

When Southerners who remained at home proved too weak to protect their property, the responsibility sometimes fell to loyal household slaves. Abram Brown, who served Virginia's Horner family, determined to guard the house while his master was off fighting in the Confederate Army. With Federal troops advancing and Lincoln's Emancipation Proclamation common knowledge in the South, Brown was offered

his liberty, but he refused. "I promised Mars Richard to stay till he come and I'm going to do it and take care of things," said Brown. And he succeeded in doing just that, right through to the armistice.

The inhabitants and the invaders were able in some felicitous instances to maintain the highest standards of behavior, despite the exigencies of the occupation. An aristocratic lady in Rappahannock County, Virginia, found her mansion surrounded by Federals, who bivouacked on her property. When the commanding general, German-born Franz Sigel, called on her with his staff, the *grande dame* rang for her servant and said, "John, tea for fourteen." The visit went off smoothly. The lady entertained the officers by singing what she called the "songs of my own land," including "The Bonnie Blue Flag" and "Dixie." And General Sigel proved that he was a true son of Germany's *musikmeisters* by performing at the piano "in grand style."

But gallant behavior on the part of Northern soldiers was the exception. Too often, undefended women found themselves confronted by soldiers demanding the keys to their cellars, their smokehouses, and any other storage places that might contain something worth taking.

"Yesterday evening we had another visit from the Lancers," wrote Judith McGuire in her diary. "They fed their horses at M's barn, ripping off the planks that the corn might roll out. The door was opened by the overseer, but that was too slow a way for thieves and robbers. While they were filling the wagons, four officers went over every part of the house, even the drawers and trunks. These men wore the trappings of officers! While I write, I have six

111

wagons in view at my brother's barn, taking off his corn, and the choice spirits accompanying them are catching the sheep and carrying them off. This robbery now goes on every day."

Mary Mallard of Georgia bitterly recorded what it was like "to see my house broken open, threatened to be burned to ashes, refused food and ordered to be starved to death, told that I had no right even to food or water, that I should be 'humbled in the very dust I walked upon,' a pistol and a carbine presented to my breast, cursed and reviled as a rebel, a hyprocrite, a devil. Every servant, on pain of having their brains blown out, forbidden to wait upon us or furnish us food. Every trunk, bureau, box, room, closet opened or broken open and searched."

Enemy looters coveted the household silver especially, and to save it Southerners came up with ingenious hiding places. Some concealed their treasures in babies' cradles, birds' nests, swamps, the beds of pregnant women or ailing grandmothers, even in outhouses. Susan Leigh Blackford, who left Richmond for Charlottesville, tested a method of hiding her silver sugar dish, cream pot, bowl, forks and spoons by tying them all in a spare pair of her husband's drawers and hanging the bundle around her waist, where it was hidden from view by her hoops. "It did well while I sat still," she reported, "but as I walked and when I sat down the clanking destroyed all hope of concealment. Of course the ridiculous side of the situation struck me and I could not restrain my laughter."

Legions of Southerners, rich and poor alike, simply took to the roads at the warning, "The Yankees are coming!" Many had no choice but to leave. General Ulysses S. Grant at one point issued a directive that would have banished from their home grounds every Southern family with a father, husband or brother in the Confederate Army. The edict — never enforced — included the widows and orphans of slain Confederate soldiers. For his part, General Sherman drove out prominent families by the dozens for their aid and comfort to the Confederate cause — or as retaliatory measures for ambush attacks on his troops. Some of these important Confederate families acquired eleventh-hour amnesty — or food and relief from pillage — by taking an oath of allegiance to the Union.

But even in defeat, many Southerners spurned conciliation: "The enemy will dole out rations if we will take the oath," reported one die-hard Southerner, adding, "but who is so base as to do that?" When an elderly Virginian named Shacklett refused the oath, Federal troops "took him out with a rope around his neck and drew him to a tree," according to one account. When the man still refused, the Federals gave in and released him.

Other Southerners fled before the threat of such treatment — or because the Yankees destroyed their homes. The wife of a pastor in Virginia described the ruination of some of her friends: "Their crops destroyed; their businesses suspended; their servants gone. How can they remain without even the present means of support, and nothing in prospect?"

Refugees who had enough time to think before leaving had to make painful decisions about which household and personal possessions to take with them on the road. Some affluent planters insisted on packing

Spurred by rumors of an imminent Federal attack, residents of Savannah, Georgia, flee the city in December 1861. The exodus proved premature: Although Union forces had taken Fort Pulaski at the mouth of the Savannah River, the city's defenses held for three more years.

The "Beast" of New Orleans

Depicted as a hyena, General Benjamin Butler shoulders a stolen spoon in this Southern cartoon. Besides being called "Beast," Butler was known as "Spoons" for his alleged yen for stealing silverware from the homes of wealthy New Orleanians.

No Northern officer was more fiercely detested in the South than Major General Benjamin F. Butler, military governor of New Orleans. This shrewd, ambitious politician from Massachusetts was embroiled in controversy from the moment he took charge of the city in May 1862.

Butler quickly moved to banish or jail Confederate activists and confiscate their property. He sparked an international furor by seizing $800,000 in hidden Confederate silver from the office of the Dutch consul. And when one citizen was so bold as to desecrate the U.S. flag in public, Butler had him hanged.

But none of Butler's actions brought him greater infamy than General Order No. 28 (below), by which he made it a crime for women to insult his soldie[rs] in public. The cleverly worded orde[r] was denounced all over the South, b[ut] it worked: The provocative insul[ts] stopped without a single woman ever b[e]ing arrested for violating the law.

Butler's iron-fisted rule produced oth[er] practical results. Under his regim[e] looting and destruction were rare. B[y] taxing the wealthy, he was able to fee[d] the poor, and in his courts of law black[s] were accorded equal status with white[s].

For all that, Butler became too contr[o]versial a figure for the Lincoln admini[s]tration, and in December 1862 he w[as] relieved of command. "I was always [a] friend of southern rights," he insiste[d] "but an enemy of southern wrongs."

Head-Quarters, Department of the Gulf, New Orleans, May 15, 1862.

General Orders, No. 28.

As the Officers and Soldiers of the United States have been subject to repeated insults from the women calling themselves ladies of New Orleans, in return for the most scrupulous non-interference and courtesy on our part, it is ordered that hereafter when any Female shall, by word, gesture, or movement, insult or show contempt for any officer or soldier of the United States, she shall be regarded and held liable to be treated as a woman of the town plying her avocation.

By command of Maj.-Gen. BUTLER,

GEORGE C. STRONG,

A. A. G. Chief of Staff.

A Northern cartoon portrays the effectiveness of Butler's order No. 28. Before the order, two hoop-skirted New Orleans ladies spit in the faces of Federal officers. But after the order (*far right*), their demeanor is more genteel.

Threatened with expulsion from the city unless they comply, New Orleanians gather at a Federal office to swear allegiance to the United States. A Northern reporter who witnessed the scene wrote that the residents faced two dreadful alternatives: "Starvation in Dixie or bowing to the horrible Yankee flag."

up all the possessions they could haul. One Charleston, South Carolina, matriarch, having set off with a wagon train full of furniture to a refuge about 60 miles away in Clarendon County, still worried that she had not taken enough. On arrival she wrote to her son back in Charleston that she would not feel "at home" until he sent on a second load consisting of "2 bedsteads with 13 slats, tester posts, 5 bundles of mahogany chairs, 2 setees, 1 desk board, 1 easy chair, 1 bundle of pillows, 1 tub, pots, foot-tubs, and 2 sofas." The wife of President Davis, fleeing south as Richmond was falling, reportedly insisted on filling two great army wagons and two ambulances with her family's personal belongings, causing the vehicles — in the words of a fellow fugitive — to "crawl along" and to leave behind "a trail like an army corps."

Those families who set off with a procession of wagons were fortunate if their conveyances — and the horses, mules and oxen pulling them — were not impressed along the way by Federal invaders or Confederate soldiers, leaving the refugees stranded by the roadside amidst their belongings. People who lacked sufficient wagons had to pay dearly to hire them. A Louisiana refugee family paid a staggering $3,000 to rent a four-horse hackney. Those without money sometimes served as their own beasts of burden, pulling handmade carts piled high with their baggage. Any workaday necessities not taken along had to be either scrounged up or done without. Lacking cooking utensils, one refugee considered herself lucky to be able to rent them at the price of a dollar per item, per month. Unable to buy cloth, a Tennessee woman on the road complained

In this sketch by a Southern artist, a drunken Federal officer holding a Confederate flag taunts a scornful Southern woman and her terrified daughter. Other soldiers maul her husband and ransack their home.

that she had to patch her baby's nightgown "one hundred times."

A few of those displaced managed to prepare on a moment's notice for the unknown road. Some just grabbed a couple of things and ran. A Baton Rouge woman, preparing to leave the city, stuffed a pillowcase mostly with frills, plus a few mementos. She itemized the contents in her diary: "four underskirts, three chemises, as many pairs of stockings, two underbodies, the prayer book father gave me, 'Tennyson' that Harry gave me when I was fourteen, two unmade muslins, a white mull, English grenadine trimmed with lilac, and a purple linen, and nightgown. Then, I must have Lavinia's daguerrotype, and how will I leave Will's when perhaps he is dead?"

The wife of Confederate General Leonidas Polk proved calm and collected in the face of an emergency departure. When she was forced to leave Nashville in February 1862, after the fall of Fort Donelson, she had only one hour to make the last civilian train out of town. Calling instructions to her children, she somehow pulled off an orderly departure with a full complement of baggage containing even the family portraits, which she had cut from their frames. The only thing she regretted leaving behind in her whirlwind exodus was the turkey dinner that had just been prepared — and about which the family dreamed with longing in the hungry days that followed.

The Polks were lucky to be on a train. In every threatened town or city, desperate citizens rushed the depots to squeeze themselves and their belongings onto the last, wheezing trains headed for the shrinking sanctuary of Confederate territory. Mary

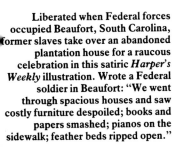

Liberated when Federal forces occupied Beaufort, South Carolina, former slaves take over an abandoned plantation house for a raucous celebration in this satiric *Harper's Weekly* illustration. Wrote a Federal soldier in Beaufort: "We went through spacious houses and saw costly furniture despoiled; books and papers smashed; pianos on the sidewalk; feather beds ripped open."

Their possessions piled high on a wagon, a family prepares to leave home before the War engulfs them. To travel in war zones, civilians were required to carry off

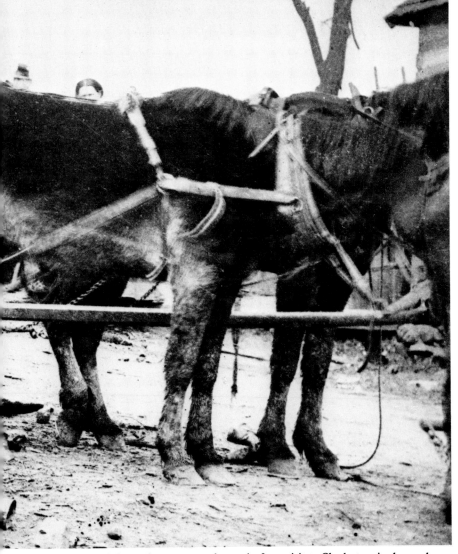

...ses issued by the Confederate Army; one such permit, for a visit to Charleston, is shown above.

Webster Loughborough of Mississippi never forgot the turmoil at the Jackson station, where she had pushed her way aboard a train for Vicksburg. The platform, she wrote, was "crowded with crushing and elbowing human beings, swaying to and fro — baggage being thrown hither and thither."

Refugee trains were pitiful sights. A newspaper reporter glimpsed one as it passed through eastern Tennessee: "Seats, aisles, platforms, baggage cars and tops of cars were covered with passengers, and thousands had been left at the depot begging to come." Along the way, trains packed with refugees were sometimes fired upon by Federal troops. Joseph Le Conte, a noted South Carolina science professor, described his rail journey: "The road is still open, but the Yanks have planted a battery within a half-a-mile of it and amuse themselves by shelling every passing car. We wait until dark and then run swiftly by the point of danger. One shell exploded directly over us, but did no damage." Such attacks were widely publicized by the Southern press, adding immeasurably to the anxiety of those citizens who felt they had to flee.

Bands of lawless stragglers and deserters also bedeviled the refugees. Some of these

A Federal officer poses with his family outside a house appropriated for their use during the occupation of New Bern, North Carolina. Such seizures of private property were not always disastrous for the owner. The Federals often took good care of the homes, and even paid for damages that occurred during their stay.

gangs, like the Unionist sympathizers led by Newton Knight, practiced their own brand of justice. But other gangs were headed by bandits of no scruples. In the outback areas of the South, such groups scoured the countryside, preying on vulnerable refugees. In western Arkansas a gang led by a cutthroat named Cullen Baker terrorized citizens, both on the roads and in their homes. The band extorted protection money and food, and did its best to prevent wayfarers and residents from leaving the area. In 1864 a group of 200 refugees and locals tried to break out of the gang's fiefdom. But Baker's renegades caught up with the fleeing party at the Saline River, shot some of its leaders and forced the rest back, murdering several more as they were herded along.

Contemplating such hazards, most uprooted Southerners preferred to remain within their own state boundaries. Expecting that the Yankees would soon be turned back, the refugees wanted to be able to return to their homes quickly. To this end, they would simply edge away from the advancing Federals, moving step by step like gypsies. But their hopes were illusory. They were forced to move farther off, and to move again, as often as a dozen times, until they despaired of regaining their old homes or finding new ones.

Living conditions on the road were often primitive and cruel. After one of many desperate days Joseph Le Conte spent on the road with his family, he wrote in his diary: "Bitter cold this morning. Water poured into the basin for face-washing freezes instantly. Ladies suffered extremely in the open wagons today. Made about 20 miles and stopped at the house of a very poor woman. She could give us shelter, but neither food nor bedding.''

A young woman fleeing Baton Rouge on foot described the roadway as "a heart-rending scene. Women searching for their babies along the road, where they had been lost; others sitting in the dust and crying and wringing their hands. All the talk was of burning homes, houses knocked to pieces by balls, famine, murder, desolation.''

Texas, of little strategic interest to the Federals, offered a haven. But people with deep roots in the Old South moved there with reluctance. The big landowners and conservative middle-class farmers of Louisiana and Mississippi, in particular, had long disdained the Lone Star State as the end of the world, plagued by heat, wind and dust. "No society above the grade of Comanches," grumbled a Louisianian, "and no schools worth sending the children to.''

Yet Texas had the virtue of being far from the enemy — an asset that droves of Southerners were quick to exploit. The eastern and central parts of the state became a microcosm of the Confederacy, as refugees from Louisiana and Mississippi found themselves thrown together with thousands from Arkansas, Missouri and Tennessee. Some families had even hazarded the trek from distant Virginia.

Houston became the major center for resettlement; in 1862 the local newspaper declared that every hotel was filled "from garret to basement," and that there were enough new settlers in the place "to whip any Yankee force." Other towns throughout the region — particularly San Antonio, Tyler, Marshall and Waco — doubled, then tripled in size.

Most of the planters and small farmers who migrated to Texas bought or rented land and set about growing food for their families. They came to accept the crude conditions and even praised the state's dry, healthy climate. But a few of the richer émigrés fussed and pined for the more elegant life they had left behind. Refugee women seemed the most offended by the coarse grain of life in the young state. One 10-year-old girl disliked the place, she wrote, because its "ladies smoke cigars, chew tobacco, take snuff and tilt back on two legs of their chairs!" Another woman reported her disgust when two Texas women she had invited to dinner asked incredulously, "You don't dip snuff, nor chew, nor nothing, do you?"

In other Confederate states — especially Virginia, the Carolinas, Alabama and Georgia — the refugees themselves became objects of disdain. Many local people treated them like outlanders rather than fellow citizens in distress. Stranded in Selma, Alabama, Kentuckian Elodie Todd, the sister of Mary Todd Lincoln, bridled at her cool reception by the locals, who seemed to think that because her home was *"not* on a *cotton plantation* there is no difference between me and a *Northerner."*

Virginians tended to be the haughtiest. Several young refugee women appeared at a church in Lynchburg, Virginia, and were curtly told by the minister to find seats in the gallery, since the pews were reserved for parishioners. Chagrined, they did as they were told, and soon joined in the singing of a hymn. Its final lines brought a smile to the lips of the newcomers and a

blush to the faces of the congregation: "Haste my soul; Oh haste away, to seats prepared above." To avoid the sting of such snobbery, some refugee women pretended to be natives of Virginia rather than acknowledge that their ancestors were not among the "first families."

Expatriates from Maryland had a particularly troublesome time in Virginia. Of the thousands who fled Maryland for the Confederacy at the beginning of the War, many adult males volunteered for the Army. But others opened profitable businesses in Virginia with the considerable funds they had brought along with them. This irritated the locals, who considered the Marylanders vulgar and opportunistic. The ill feeling extended even to wounded soldiers in hospital wards: In one instance, Phoebe Yates Pember, matron of Richmond's Chimborazo Hospital, had to have Maryland wounded shifted to a separate ward to stop the harassment they were receiving from Virginia convalescents.

Elsewhere in the Confederacy, public-spirited citizens tried to counteract the harshness of local chauvinism. An editor in Columbia, South Carolina, published a strong protest entitled "Refugee Haters." It indicted South Carolina's citizenry for indifference to the pilgrims who crowded the state, going so far as to compare Southern householders unfavorably to "the Yankees," who, "as bad as they are, have some sense of what they owe their kind."

But even those Southerners who tried to extend a welcome to fugitive friends, relatives and strangers found the unending procession hard to bear when their houses and neighborhoods grew more congested and food vanished. "The refugees eat up pretty much everything that is raised in the neighborhood," wrote a distraught Charleston man to his wife, while a woman from Charlotte confided to her son that she had begun to dread "to hear the doorbell ring." By 1864 Secretary of War James Seddon noted that refugees were now regarded less with "sympathy than apprehension, for they are looked upon as diminishing the means and increasing the privations of the communities to which they flee."

As the Federal armies rolled forward, more and more refugees crowded into the cities along the Atlantic Coast and in the Piedmont. This exodus to Richmond, Atlanta, Mobile, Savannah and Columbia was made by a people whose roots were on the farm. An Atlanta reporter wondered why "refugees insist on swarming around crowded cities, when the country offers so much better and cheaper retreat." And in fact, real-estate agents filled the papers with advertisements headed "Refugees!" and offering fine country places at knockdown prices. Yet despite inadequate housing and food shortages, the refugees were better able to find work — as well as up-to-date news and diverse company — in the cities.

From the onset of the War, Richmond was the main refugee center. Originally a quiet community of nearly 40,000 souls, the Confederate capital doubled in population during the first year of the fighting, and continued to grow thereafter.

Thousands of the displaced came to Richmond hoping for employment in the sprawling national and state bureaucracies. Others — particularly the more well-to-do refugees — flocked there to sample the capital's unflagging round of bittersweet parties and balls, to mingle in high government and

Set free by the Federal conquest of South Carolina's Sea Islands, former slaves enjoy an idyllic independence on Hilton Head Island in this romanticized pai

than 10,000 slaves eventually found refuge on the islands dotting the coasts of South Carolina and Georgia.

military circles, and to renew acquaintances with other blue-blooded émigrés. A reporter strolling down Main Street and observing crowds of refugees found it easy to imagine himself walking "among the throngs of Broadway." By day, jousting tournaments presided over by refugee belles were held in the nearby countryside. By night, elaborate *soirées* cast gay candlelight onto Richmond's swarming streets.

Some of the new arrivals were repelled by such indulgences at a time when Confederate soldiers were being slaughtered on the battlefields. A refugee walking home one evening passed a mansion ablaze with laughter and dancing. "I thought of the gayety of Paris during the French Revolution," she mused, "of the ball at Brussels the night before the battle of Waterloo."

The gaiety was tempered by a sense of foreboding. Sara Pryor of Richmond remarked, "The soldier danced with the lady of his love at night," for on the next day he faced "the dance of death." And so it proved to be: In one of Richmond's most brilliant wartime social events, Baltimore belle Hetty Cary was married to Brigadier General John Pegram in January 1865. A grand crowd of Confederate officers and their ladies attended the splendid wedding. A scant three weeks later many of the same friends assembled at graveside to bury the handsome 33-year-old general, killed at Hatcher's Run near Petersburg.

For the ordinary people among the refugees — farmers, mechanics, laborers and merchants — there was no relief at all from the desperate struggle for existence. Judith McGuire recounted the story of an unfortunate young mother: "Her name is Brown; her husband had been a workman in Freder-

icksburg. He joined the army, and was killed at the second battle of Manassas. Many of her acquaintances in Fredericksburg fled last winter during the bombardment; she became alarmed, and with her three children fled too."

The widow Brown could not find enough work in Richmond to support her family, so a kindly neighbor provided her a room rent free. A scrubby garden plot yielded some turnip tops, which she boiled and fed to the children.

When asked if this satisfied their hunger, the gaunt fugitive answered, "Well, it is something to go upon for awhile, but it does not stick by us like as bread does, and then we gets hungry again, and I am afraid to let the children eat them too often, lest they should get sick; so I tries to get them to go to sleep; and sometimes the woman in the next room will bring the children her leavings, but she is monstrous poor."

A few days following this conversation, Judith McGuire, outraged that a Confederate soldier's widow and family were slowly starving in the Confederate capital, went back to help. But the woman and her children had vanished.

Judith McGuire herself had been in dire need of shelter and assistance when she first settled in Richmond in 1862. A resourceful and determined woman, she was wellborn and well connected — married to a distinguished clergyman, and close friends with her prewar neighbors, General and Mrs. Lee. Nevertheless, she and her husband had to scramble with the rest after they fled Alexandria for Richmond.

The Reverend McGuire found work as a postal clerk, and Mrs. McGuire trudged the streets for weeks searching for a room

Charting a Bold Course to Freedom

In Charleston Harbor on May 12, 1862, the officers of the Confederate steamer *Planter* left the vessel in the care of their best crewman, a slave named Robert Smalls, and disembarked for a night ashore. It was a fateful move, for Smalls and fellow slaves left aboard had been waiting for an opportunity to execute an audacious and long-cherished plan—a bolt for freedom.

Smalls, 22 years old, was one of the most skilled seamen in Charleston. But he knew that it would take more than good seamanship to sneak a warship out of a fortified harbor.

Donning an officer's coat and the captain's distinctive broad-brimmed straw hat, Smalls got under way about 3 a.m. and guided the ship slowly down the harbor in the darkness. As planned, he stopped briefly to pick up his family and those of his crewmen. Then he steered the ship adroitly through a gantlet of Confederate harbor forts. But by dawn, the terrible guns of Fort Sumter still lay ahead: Smalls would have to bluff his way past the fort in full daylight.

As the *Planter* chugged under Fort Sumter's powerful batteries, Smalls gave the pass signal with the ship's whistle and, keeping to the shadows in the pilothouse, waved to the sentinel. The guard thought he recognized the familiar figure in the straw hat; he cheered the ship on: "Blow the damned Yankees to hell, and bring one of them in!"

"Aye, Aye," Smalls called back.

Once beyond the range of the fort's guns, Smalls lowered the Confederate flag, hoisted a white bed sheet, and turned his prize over to a Federal blockade ship. He explained to the astonished Federal sailors: "I thought the *Planter* might be of some use to Uncle Abe."

SEAMAN ROBERT SMALLS

The *Planter*, shown here in a heavily retouched photograph, was outfitted during the War with a 32-pound pivot gun and a 24-pound howitzer.

with cooking privileges. Time after time she met with disappointment. At last she discovered a back room on the third floor of a private house, but the cold-eyed landlady there demanded an exorbitant rent — just three dollars less than her husband's entire monthly salary.

Again she set out on her search and eventually found a tiny room in a school building that had been converted into a lodging house. Despite the Southern bias against gentlewomen doing salaried work, she took a job in the office of the Commissary-General for wages of $125 a month. Although this was soon increased to $250, inflation was rapidly devouring the value of Confederate currency. In March of 1863, butter was $3.50 a pound; by February of 1864, it was $25 a pound. A bushel of corn meal, which had earlier sold for $6, now brought $20. A barrel of flour fetched up to $300, a pound of coffee $50. In the process, the estimated yearly cost of feeding a family had climbed to a forbidding $4,800.

But the McGuires made do. They moved again, this time to the village of Ashland, on the outskirts of Richmond. Here they shared a cottage with four other families, and the couple traveled by train to the city. In her spare time, Judith McGuire worked through church organizations to help the most destitute families in the city and also acted as nurse to wounded soldiers in Richmond hospitals. She even continued her eloquent diary after writing paper gave out — using brown wrapping paper.

The problems of refugee life were onerously compounded for blacks. Slaves were offered little choice about where to go or what to do. They were forced either to remain on the plantation or to flee with their masters — although some did so out of loyalty rather than duress.

Many slaves became confused or downright terrified by the conflicting demands placed on them. "One night there'd be a gang of Secesh, and the next one, there'd come along a gang of Yankees," a former Arkansas slave recalled. "Pa was 'fraid of both of 'em. Secesh said they'd kill him if he left his white folks. Yankees said they'd kill him if he didn't leave 'em."

Some planters became just as frightened and demoralized, to the point that they simply departed, leaving behind their slaves — and everything else.

Calmer, more profit-minded owners tried selling off their slaves, beginning with those who were difficult to manage. But prices fluctuated wildly, depending on local supply and demand, inflation, or how the Confederate Army was fairing. With the Federal victories at Gettysburg and Vicksburg in July 1863, more and more masters became willing to unload their slaves at any price. When Virginia's old archsecessionist Edmund Ruffin, who had fired the first shot at Fort Sumter, auctioned off 15 of his slaves, his son explained that they were "all consumers and were sold on account of the expense of keeping and the doubtful tenure of the property."

Other planters tried to keep their slaves by sending them into the back country, under their own overseers or those of friends. Louis Manigault dispatched 10 blacks from his coastal Georgia plantation — the ones he considered "most likely would cause trouble" — to an upcountry farm "remote from all excitement." Mary Chesnut reported that one of her wealthy friends sought a safe place for 200 slaves who "had grown to be a nuisance."

Often, however, when blacks learned that their masters were planning to send them away, they ran away instead. When South Carolina's John Berkley Grimball made inquiries in Charleston about a place to relocate himself and his possessions, the slaves got wind of it. Two days later Grimball awoke to discover that 80 of his hands — including "the best of them" — had vanished. "Negro property is a most unmanageable property and has been our ruin," lamented his son.

Even among those slaves who harbored a deep personal loyalty toward their masters, the urge for freedom could be overpowering. Such was the case with a black body servant who, at the battle of Antietam, first risked his life to rescue his wounded master from the field, then risked it again to flee across Federal lines.

Sometimes runaways were bitterly disillusioned by their reception, for the Federal Army could not support the throng of black refugees, even on half rations. Furthermore, Northern troops often handled them roughly. "Many, very many of the soldiers and not a few of the officers," wrote a war correspondent for the *New York Evening Post*, "have habitually treated the negroes with the coarsest and most brutal insolence and inhumanity; never speaking to them but to curse and revile them."

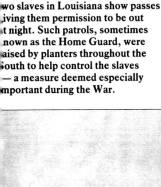

Intercepted by a plantation patrol, two slaves in Louisiana show passes giving them permission to be out at night. Such patrols, sometimes known as the Home Guard, were raised by planters throughout the South to help control the slaves — a measure deemed especially important during the War.

Forlorn memorials to a lost era, six tall chimneys jutting from a grove in rural Virginia mark the site of a once-elegant country home and its outbuildings.

Charlotte Forten, a teacher who arrived on Hilton Head Island in 1862 to open a school for former slaves, was dismayed to find that the occupying officers there "talked flippantly, and sneeringly of the negroes, using an epithet more offensive than gentlemanly." In Norfolk, Virginia, a freedwoman wrote of seeing fellow blacks abused "in every possible way" — property destroyed or stolen, men beaten, women raped — and summed up her feelings with the lament: "I reckon I'm Massa Lincoln's slave now."

Perhaps the hardest road of all, for slaves and masters alike, was the long trail west into Texas. Well over 150,000 slaves from Mississippi and Louisiana alone made the difficult journey afoot under the supervision of masters or overseers. Others slogged as far as 1,000 miles from central Georgia, the Carolinas or Virginia. The slaves remembered it, in the words of one freedman, Charley Williams, as "the awfullest trip any man ever make!" Often, those on the trek were harried by soldiers or stragglers from both sides. "We had to hide from everybody until we find out if they Yankees or Secesh," Williams recalled. "We go along little old back roads and up one mountain and down another, through the woods all the way." Many of the old and feeble were buried along the way, victims of fever, exhaustion and starvation.

The vast uprooting of the South's peoples, black and white, was one of the most devastating traumas of the Civil War. In trying to escape the indignity and uncertainty of life under military occupation, refugees were merely subjected to another ordeal: the hostility, hardships and dangers of a tortuous journey.

131

To Throw Off Slavery's Bonds

Early in the War, Dora Franks, a house slave on a large Mississippi plantation, overheard a fateful conversation between her master and mistress: "He said he feared all the slaves would be took. She said if that was true she feel like jumping in the well. I hate to hear her say that, but from that minute I started praying for freedom."

To cast off a lifetime of bondage and take control of their destinies as free men and women was the fervent prayer of the more than three million slaves living in the South when the War began. Booker T. Washington recalled that when he was a young slave in Virginia his elders would gather in their cabins late at night to discuss the War and what it might mean. "Even the most ignorant members of my race on the remote plantations," he wrote, "felt in their hearts that the freedom of the slaves would be the one great result of the War if the Northern armies conquered."

So profound was the slaves' yearning for freedom that when Federal soldiers finally appeared, many likened the event to the Biblical coming of the Kingdom of Heaven. One slave woman preparing a Sunday dinner within earshot of the Manassas battlefield greeted each cannon blast with a grateful "Ride on, Massa Jesus." And when Federal troops entered Charleston, South Carolina, in 1865, a 69-year-old slave who had waited for freedom all her life remembered feeling that day "nearer to Heaven than I ever felt before."

Five generations of a slave family, all born on the same plantation near Beaufort, South Carolina, assemble for a portrait. They were among 10,000 slaves abandoned by their masters when Federal troops occupied the area in November 1861.

KINGDOM COMING.

Copied by permission of ROOT & CADY, Music Publishers, 95 Clark St., Chicago, owners of the copyright. As sung by DAN BRYANT

Say, darkeys, hab you seen de massa,
 Wid de muffstash on his face,
Go long de road some time dis mornin',
 Like he gwine to leab de place?
He seen a smoke way up de ribber,
 Whar de Linkum gunboats lay;
He took his hat, an' lef' berry sudden,
 An' I spec' he's run away!

Chorus—De massa run? ha, ha!
 De darkey stay? ho, ho!
 It mus' be now de kingdom comin'
 An' de year Jubilo!

He six foot one way' two foot tudder,
 An, he weigh t'ree hundred pound,
His coat so big, he couldn't pay de tailor,
 An' it won't go half way round.
He drill so much, dey call him Cap'an,
 An' he get so drefful tanned,
I spec' he try an' fool dem Yankees,
 For to tink he's contraband.   Chorus.

De darkeys feel so berry lonesom,
 Libing in de log-House on de lawn,
Dey move dar tings to massa's parlor,
 For to keep it while he's gone,
Dars wine an' cider in de kitchen,
 An' de darkeys dey'll hab some;
I spose dey'll all be cornfiscated,
 When de Linkum sojers come.   Chorus.

De oberseer he make us trouble,
 An' he dribe us round a spell,
We lock him up in the smoke-House cellar,
 Wid de key trown in de well.
De whip is lost, de han-cuff broken,
 But de massa'll hab his pay,
He's ole enuff, big enuff, ought to know better
 Dan to went an' run away.   Chorus.

Traveling by oxcart, a slave family makes good its escape from bondage in August 1862 by reaching the Rappahannock River in Virginia, where a Federal army was camped. The War prompted thousands of slaves to desert their plantations and flee toward Federal lines.

Two ragged young runaways from a Louisiana plantation sit for their portrait in Federally occupied Baton Rouge. During the War that city became a haven for thousands of fugitive slaves who poured in from the surrounding countryside.

The Rupture of Fragile Loyalties

Wherever Federal troops secured a foothold in the South, the institution of slavery crumbled. On the Sea Islands of South Carolina, planters fled at the first approach of Federal gunboats in the fall of 1861: Their slaves were declared "contraband of war" and put to work picking cotton for wages paid from the Federal Treasury.

As so-called contrabands, slaves were wards of the Federal government and were not destined to gain freedom legally until President Lincoln proclaimed emancipation in 1863. In fact, they were treated by the Federals as free men — a distinction that blacks held in bondage in other parts of the country quickly grasped. In the Confederate West, many planters took an oath of loyalty to the Union, expecting the Army to enforce slave discipline. But so many slaves bolted that Federal commanders had to set up huge contraband camps to cope with the exodus.

The proximity of Federal troops invariably undermined the authority of those planters whose slaves did not flee. Traditional loyalties based on generations of mutual dependence between master and servant disintegrated overnight. The sudden breakup of the old order — coupled with a common belief among white Southerners that their "peculiar institution" actually benefited blacks — left many masters indignant at their "betrayal" by "ungrateful" slaves. Indeed, when Tennessee planter John Bills's hands quit work altogether after the Federals arrived, slaveholders all over the South could echo his lament: "We are being deprived of that Control needful to make them happy and prosperous."

At Hilton Head, South Carolina, slaves liberated by the Federal occupation in 1861 sort cotton on a confiscated plantation for wages of 25 cents a day plus rations. Treasury Bureau agents sent from Washington supervised the harvest, which was sold to raise Federal revenues.

Newly liberated slaves, some wearing castoff Federal Army uniforms, cultivate their own sweet-potato patch on a Hilton Head Island plantation. Governm

...horities encouraged such enterprise, both to increase food production and to motivate the former slaves to work for their own benefit.

Slaves on a Sea Island plantation gather beneath a huge oak tree to hear a Federal agent read the proclamation declaring them "thenceforth and forever fr

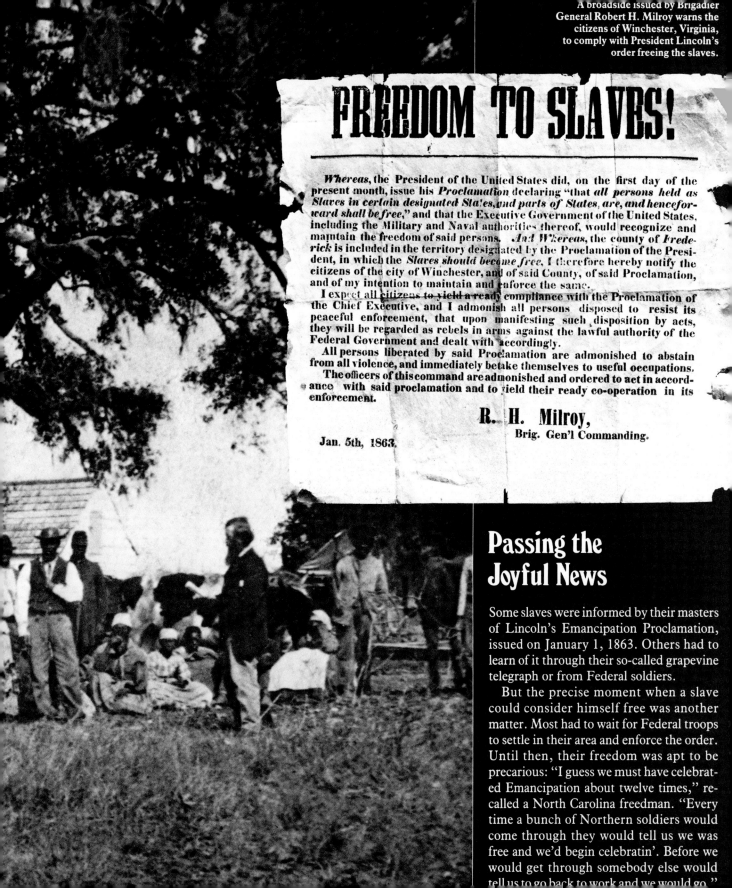

FREEDOM TO SLAVES!

Whereas, the President of the United States did, on the first day of the present month, issue his *Proclamation* declaring "that *all persons held as Slaves in certain designated States, and parts of States, are, and henceforward shall be free*," and that the Executive Government of the United States, including the Military and Naval authorities thereof, would recognize and maintain the freedom of said persons. *And Whereas*, the county of *Frederick* is included in the territory designated by the Proclamation of the President, in which the *Slaves should become free*, I therefore hereby notify the citizens of the city of Winchester, and of said County, of said Proclamation, and of my intention to maintain and enforce the same.

I expect all citizens to yield a ready compliance with the Proclamation of the Chief Executive, and I admonish all persons disposed to resist its peaceful enforcement, that upon manifesting such disposition by acts, they will be regarded as rebels in arms against the lawful authority of the Federal Government and dealt with accordingly.

All persons liberated by said Proclamation are admonished to abstain from all violence, and immediately betake themselves to useful occupations.

The officers of this command are admonished and ordered to act in accordance with said proclamation and to yield their ready co-operation in its enforcement.

R. H. Milroy,
Brig. Gen'l Commanding.

Jan. 5th, 1863.

Passing the Joyful News

Some slaves were informed by their masters of Lincoln's Emancipation Proclamation, issued on January 1, 1863. Others had to learn of it through their so-called grapevine telegraph or from Federal soldiers.

But the precise moment when a slave could consider himself free was another matter. Most had to wait for Federal troops to settle in their area and enforce the order. Until then, their freedom was apt to be precarious: "I guess we must have celebrated Emancipation about twelve times," recalled a North Carolina freedman. "Every time a bunch of Northern soldiers would come through they would tell us we was free and we'd begin celebratin'. Before we would get through somebody else would tell us to go back to work and we would go."

Kate Foote, a Connecticut volunteer sent to Beaufort, South Carolina, in 1862 by the New England Freedman's Aid Society, teaches two of her charges a grammar lesson. The slaves, one instructor recalled, "had seen the magic of a scrap of writing and were eager to share such power."

"The Next Best Thing to Liberty"

"If I do nothing more while I live," vowed freedman Charles Whiteside, "I shall give my children a chance to go to school."

Thousands of former slaves of all ages enrolled in schools set up by Northern missionaries and teachers who followed the troops southward. To people whose memories of the lash were still vivid, the schoolhouse was a symbol of freedom and a guarantee against a return to slavery. A teacher in North Carolina reported that his pupils would "endure any penance rather than be deprived of this privilege." And for his part, Charles Whiteside deemed education "the next best thing to liberty."

Freedmen gather outside a school building in Beaufort, one of 30 schools established for former slaves on the Sea Islands by Northern benevolent associations. By the end of the War, more than 9,000 freedmen were attending classes along the South Carolina coast.

From Slave to Soldier

"Let the black man get upon his person the brass letters, U.S.," abolitionist Frederick Douglass declared, "let him get an eagle on his button, and a musket on his shoulder and bullets in his pocket, and there is no power on earth which can deny that he has earned the right to citizenship."

Such sentiment went unheeded by the U.S. government early in the War. Although the Army did employ thousands of the contrabands then massed behind its fortifications or serving as cooks. Then in August 1862, the War Department announced that it would begin recruiting former slaves for garrison duty and to man naval vessels. In November, black soldiers were mustered into the Army — the first of an estimated 186,000 who would serve during the War. The decision to employ black troops shocked the Confederacy. Declared one anxious citizen, "If the slaves will make

On the day President Lincoln signed the Emancipation Proclamation, black soldiers of the 1st South Carolina Volunteers assemble at Port Royal. Two mo

er their regiment had become the first unit of former slaves to be mustered into the United States Army.

End to the Dream

Through the summer of 1864, as the weight of three years of war bore down upon the tattered Confederacy, realistic people in the South lost hope for the cause. The Union now controlled the Mississippi River. Federal troops occupied much of Tennessee, together with portions of Mississippi, Georgia, South Carolina and Florida. The Confederate Army had eroded in strength to barely 150,000 men, and this weary and ill-equipped force faced an enemy one and a half times their number.

Every month, the news from the field worsened. The Army of Tennessee, under General Joseph E. Johnston, was falling back across Georgia toward Atlanta. Rear-echelon critics dubbed Johnston "the Great Retreater," and President Davis sent him an angry cable: "Will you surrender Atlanta without a fight?" Mary Chesnut recorded the grim assessment that "our all depends on that Army at Atlanta. If that fails us, the game is up." At last, disgusted by Johnston's overcautious tactics, Davis summarily replaced him with the pugnacious General John B. Hood — who had been so sorely wounded that he had lost a leg and the use of one arm, and now had to be tied to his horse when he took the field.

In Richmond, anxiety mounted as the boom of Federal cannon drew closer. Little more than 20 miles to the south, at Petersburg, 5,400 men under General Beauregard faced 16,000 Federals. There the Union's troops settled into a siege ring that began slowly to squeeze the remaining blood out of the Confederates.

In August, word arrived that 18 Federal warships had succeeded in breaking into Mobile Bay, closing the crucial port of Mobile to Confederate blockade runners. And suddenly in September came the worst tidings of all. Atlanta had fallen. President Lincoln was urging that Northern churches proclaim a day of thanksgiving. In her diary, Mary Chesnut penned a grim notation: "There is no hope."

Indeed, Southern prospects were abysmal. Great Britain, a potential ally early in the War, had soured on the Confederacy as the defeats accumulated and now, "under professions of neutrality," as Davis noted sardonically, began seizing ships that were being built for the South in English ports. The Federal blockade grew ever tighter, choking off Southern trade and supplies. As goods grew scarcer, inflation ran rampant: More than $700 million circulating in legal Confederate paper money was worth perhaps a fortieth its face value in real purchasing power.

The shortage of men in arms was devastating. "Without some increase of our strength," admitted Lee, "I cannot see how we are to escape the natural military consequences of the enemy's numerical superiority." Yet it seemed that the well of manpower had run dry. No longer were there any volunteers for service, and conscription was being evaded with universal hostility and

The Confederate attempt to negotiate peace in February 1865 is ridiculed in this Northern cartoon, depicting Vice President Alexander Stephens and his emissaries as haggard, tearful children being welcomed back to the fold by a towering Abraham Lincoln. The cartoon was captioned, "Flying to Abraham's Bosom."

thoroughness. "From one end of the Confederacy to the other," complained Superintendent of Conscription John S. Preston, "every constituted authority, every officer, every man and woman is engaged in opposing the enrolling officer in the execution of his duties."

In desperation, the government began to draft boys 14 to 18 years old to serve in a junior reserve, and men from 45 to 60 years old to make up a senior reserve. Although these enlistees were assigned rearguard duty to free others for action, such a move was ominous. As one chronicler put it, the South was "robbing the cradle and the grave to supply Lee's army."

By now, a large part of the South lay in ruins. The foraging armies of both sides had stripped the crops from the fields, appropriated stores of food and made off with whatever livestock they could lay their hands on. Plantation fences were torn down and used for firewood; implements rusted; houses and outbuildings deteriorated because there were no workmen on hand to maintain them — and no nails available to shore them up.

"The whole country here is a perfect waste, not a ear of corn scarcely to be found," lamented a planter from Port Gibson, Mississippi. A North Carolinian at home wrote to his brother in the Army, "I would advise you to go to the other side whear you can get plenty and not stay in this one horse barefooted naked and famine stricken Southern Confederacy."

The specter of starvation loomed over the once-bountiful land, and drove those threatened by it to desperate action. "Families are killing people's cows wherever they can get hold of them," recorded a Flori-

da judge. Outside Thomasville, Georgia, a handful of women wielding rifles held up a wagon to get three sacks of flour. More than a dozen Alabama women brandishing guns, pistols, knives and wagon tongues raided a mill and absconded with all the flour they could carry. In Kentucky, according to a contemporary account, "a party of over one hundred citizen guerrillas entered Mayfield and, after pillaging the stores and severely wounding one of the citizens, left, carrying away their booty."

For some, the most frightening element of the Confederacy's collapse was the prospect of slave insurrection. This grim vision had long haunted whites in the South. Now emancipation, proclaimed by Lincoln and enforced by the advancing Federal armies, made the nightmare seem imminent.

Die-hard Confederate leaders fed the fear in an effort to stir up a last-ditch will to fight. Davis already had announced that the Union's troops fully intended "to incite servile insurrection and light the fires of incendiarism wherever they can reach your homes, and debauch the inferior race by promising indulgence of the vilest passions as the price of treachery." He hinted ominously of approaching "atrocities from which death itself is a welcome escape."

The note of hysteria was echoed by Mississippi Governor-elect Charles Clark, who proffered a warning that "the elevation of the black race to a position of equality — aye, of superiority, will make them masters and rulers." Not long after, the Charleston *Mercury* ranted: "The poor man is reduced to the level of a nigger, his wife and daughters are to be hustled on the street by black wenches, their equals. Swaggering buck niggers are to ogle them and elbow them. Gra-

Federal military police question a pair of Virginia farmers suspected of aiding Confederate troops. For civilians caught up in battle zones, summary arrests were commonplace — particularly after Federal setback when, said one Southerner, "we felt their rod with ten fold severity."

cious God, is this what our brave soldiers are fighting for?"

As local and national authority in the South ebbed away, there were just enough incidents of slaves turning on their masters to keep fears at a high level. Emma Holmes of Charlestown trembled at the story of the killing of her old friend William Allen, "who was chopped to pieces in his barn." Another chronicle from South Carolina told of a Mrs. Allston and her daughter, who were surrounded on their plantation by a crowd of howling slaves. The blacks danced about their mistress and her daughter brandishing rice hoes, pitchforks, guns and hickory sticks, and chanting: "I free, I free, I free as a frog." Somehow, the women stayed calm and managed to extricate themselves from the situation.

In one gruesome case, an Alabama planter accompanied by Federal soldiers returned to his home to be greeted by the spectacle of about 150 rejoicing slaves; they paraded beside a wagon that bore the remains of their murdered overseer swaddled in a flag. "It appears that he had been attacked by five of them while he was at dinner," the planter recorded, "his head being split open by blows with a hatchet, and penetrated by shots at his face."

In reality, more blacks than whites died in racial strife during the slow, grinding misery of the Confederacy's final year. A number were slain for imagined or real acts of defiance. When Federal warships approached Edisto Island, off the coast of South Carolina, the island's planters evacuated to the mainland, leaving their slaves behind. Later, when a Confederate raiding party tried to remove some of the slaves, black women resisted "so violently," in the words of a local white, that the raiders "were obliged to shoot some of them."

The relentless depredation, hunger and turmoil produced in the Southern people an almost universal yearning for peace at any price, even defeat. "If it is as the newspapers say," Mary Chesnut noted, "why waste our blood? Why should we fight and die when it is no use?"

"Would that the *men* would take matters in their own hands, and end the war," another Southerner declared. "Let every man in both armies desert and go home!" North Carolina politician James Leach was bold enough to issue a public call for peace negotiations with the North: "Should we not offer the olive branch?" Vice President Alexander Stephens endorsed that sentiment wholeheartedly, issuing his own call for an end to hostilities. "Our strength and resources are exhausted," he proclaimed to a crowd in Augusta, Georgia, "and peace ought to be made."

Despite the erosion of resolve on the home front, and the imminence of military defeat, President Davis refused to negotiate without a guarantee from the North of full independence for the Confederacy and the preservation of her "institutions" — meaning slavery. On three occasions during the previous year, Davis had permitted informal approaches to the Union regarding a possible settlement of the War, but always on those strict conditions. The Federal government refused even to receive such overtures, and Davis was quick to inform the people of Lincoln's intractable stand: "Have we not been apprised by that despot that we can only expect his gracious pardon by emancipating all our slaves, swearing obedience to him and his proclamations, and becoming in point of fact the slaves of our own negroes?" Davis concluded: "The purpose of the enemy is to refuse all terms to the South except absolute, unconditional subjugation or extermination."

Striving to put the best possible face on the Confederate predicament, Davis reminded the people that General Grant, with his masses of well-fed soldiers, had been unable to break either the defensive line or the will of Lee's superbly led army during the developing sieges of Richmond and Petersburg. In the fighting, Confederate troops had inflicted more than 40,000 casualties. Davis argued that as a result, war-weariness in the North was more severe than in the Confederacy. If Southerners would only fight on a little longer — perhaps until Lee had engineered one more of his battlefield miracles — then Lincoln might be forced to sue for peace and concede their independence. Meanwhile, Davis' own policy would remain one of toughness, not conciliation — toward both the Union and dissenters on the home front. For a brief time, he seemed to get some support.

"One alternative now remains," wrote a Southern diarist, "and that is for the President to assume all power, temporarily. A dictator might be able to prevent the people from destroying themselves, and it seems that nothing short of extreme measures can prevent it."

Davis did take harsh steps to quell what he perceived to be an insidious internal threat to the Confederacy. For some time the South had been seething with rumors of subversive organizations devoted to the overthrow of the Confederacy and the restoration of peace under Union domination. Their nefarious methods, according to one report, were "the encouragement of desertion, resistance to conscription, and perhaps other designs still more dangerous." These alleged shadow groups had names attached to them such as the Peace and Constitutional Society, the Order of the Heroes of America, and the Peace

DECEMBER 1861

DECEMBER 1862

Society. And their membership was said to include men of high position: A dossier on one secret society credited it with "three justices of the peace, one Methodist minister, a prominent lawyer and an elected sheriff."

The members of one such cabal, Secretary of War Seddon asserted, were "forming a new State of Southwest Virginia, and have elected officers whom they style governor, lieutenant-governor, brigadier-general and judges." At one point, the conspiracy was believed to have spread to the front line of the Confederate Army before Richmond. An investigator stated that "most of the men of the Fifty-fourth Virginia regiment belonged to the order and all of the Twenty-second had been initiated."

To ferret out these groups and their leaders, the government enlisted the services of perhaps half a dozen detectives; but whether they uncovered anything of substance is a matter of conjecture. One investigator looking into the supposed Peace Society conced-

ed that "it is a society without officers, a community without members. No records are kept." Nevertheless, this same detective made a great point of describing the shadowy society's system of internal communication: Members would greet each other with the passwords, "I dreamed the boys are all coming home." Identification, continued the detective, was further confirmed by a handshake in which the thumb was held off to the side, to the accompaniment of the following recitation:

"What is that?"

"A grip."

"A grip of what?"

"A constitutional peace grip."

"Has it a name?"

"It has."

"Will you give it to me?

And so the litany went, through a total of 14 phrases, until security had been thoroughly established. If, despite all such precautions, a member was arrested, he could

As the War progressed, the Confederacy (*tan*) yielded more and more territory (*dark*) to the Union (*blue*). **In December 1861, the Union held only parts of Virginia and a few isolated coastal forts. In 1863, the Federal conquest of the Mississippi River removed vast sections** (*stippled*) **from all but the barest contact with Richmond. By the end of 1864, after General Sherman's march to the sea** (*arrow*), **only portions of three states — South Carolina, North Carolina and Virginia — remained in Confederate control.**

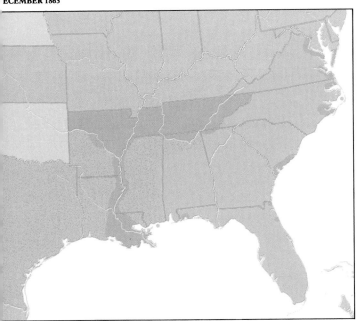

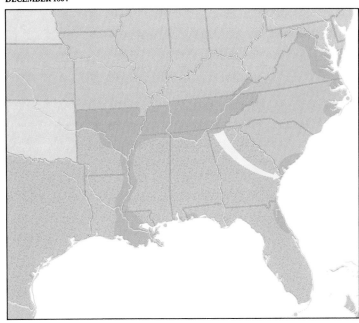

escape by repeating the phrase "Oh, Washington" three times (another report said four times), providing the jailer happened to be a fellow member.

Other detectives investigated the outlandish claim that the Order of the Heroes of America, to which both Abraham Lincoln and Ulysses S. Grant supposedly belonged, was responsible not only for the Confederate defeat at Missionary Ridge, but also the surrender of Vicksburg. Furthermore, the rumor went, Federal officers were recruiting Confederate stragglers into the order by promising them "participation in the division of the real estate of the loyal Confederate citizens."

Many such tales, but few hard facts, emerged during the investigation into the existence of the secret leagues. Nevertheless, Jefferson Davis proved adept at convincing Congress that there did exist "treasonable design." He was so persuasive in making his case, in fact, that an alarmed legislature

granted his request to suspend habeas corpus for the third time. Whether the Confederate President Davis actually believed in the existence of such subversive organizations is questionable. But suspension of habeas corpus gave him a lever by which he could exert tight control over the increasingly shaky home front. It also earned him renewed acrimony. Among the people and their various state governments, anger at Davis' regime exploded the moment he signed into law this new and final suspension of civil rights.

"Georgians, behold your chains!" thundered a black-bordered notice in the Athens *Southern Watchman*. The relentless Governor Brown reminded Davis that "this is not the constitutional liberty which so many Georgians have died to defend." Brown led his own legislature in the passage of a unanimous resolution condemning the suspension. Further, the edict required judges in Georgia to grant writs of habeas corpus to those imprisoned — or pay a fine of $2,500 to the defendant.

The legislatures of Mississippi and Louisiana passed their own hostile resolutions, while that of North Carolina nullified the suspension outright. Vice President Stephens again turned on his chief. "When the government undertakes to close the courts," he wrote, "they virtually declare war against the people."

This controversy stiffened the will of state leaders to place the needs of their home states first and end the devastation within their own borders — even if it meant breaking away from the Confederacy. William Holden, editor of the Raleigh, North Carolina, *Standard*, noted in his journal that scores of

rallies had been held across the state calling for negotiations with the North "with a view to separation." In an editorial Holden argued bluntly that his state should stay in the Confederacy only so long "as it is to the interest of North Carolina to do so, and no longer." He went so far as to call for a statewide convention to petition the Union to accept North Carolina on the guarantee that the state would retain all its old rights. Governor Vance, though frequently at odds with Holden, conceded privately that the discontent among his people was such that it might be "perhaps impossible to remove except by making some effort at negotiation with the enemy."

More strident warnings came from Geor-

Federal soldiers and freed slaves line the porch of Brierfield, Jefferson Davis' Mississippi plantation home, derisively decorated with red, white and blue bunting and a mocking epigram. On July 4, 1864, Federals hosted a picnic on the plantation grounds for Davis' former slaves.

gia, where Henry Cleveland, the influential editor of the Augusta *Constitutionalist*, advocated that Georgia save itself. Cleveland wrote Vice President Stephens, "I am satisfied the immediate secession of Georgia from the Confederate States would be the best thing we could do."

Cleveland and others placed the blame for the disintegration of the Confederacy squarely on Davis and his Cabinet. Cleveland complained that the administration would take "our Cause beyond the hand of resurrection." Confederate Congressman William Boyce of South Carolina derided "the incredible incompetency of our Executive." For his part, Jefferson Davis remained outwardly oblivious to such attacks. But privately he deplored the "persistent interference by some state authorities, Legislative, Executive and Judicial, hindering the action of the government."

By all signs, that interference would not soon abate. With many of Lee's troops in rags and shuffling around barefoot, Governor Zebulon Vance withheld from the Army 92,000 uniforms and huge stores of blankets and shoe leather, reserving the lot for his North Carolina militia.

Still more destructive was the initiative taken by Georgia's Governor Brown. After the fall of Atlanta, Brown stunned the Confederacy with his abrupt order recalling the 10,000-man Georgia militia attached to the Army of Tennessee: "I have this day withdrawn you from the command of General J. B. Hood." As insurance against any effort by General Hood to hold the men, Brown added, "I therefore hereby order and direct that each and every officer and soldier in the division have a furlough of thirty days." Moreover, Brown announced that he was contemplating a more drastic move; in his self-proclaimed role as commander in chief of every state citizen then in Confederate uniform, he weighed an order that would direct "all the sons of Georgia to return to their own State and within her own limits to rally around her glorious flag."

At about the same time, Alabama's Governor Thomas Watts announced that he would not allow any state militiamen then within Alabama to be called to duty beyond its borders. Governor Charles Clark of Mississippi followed suit with the announcement that "the State of Mississippi has to defend herself in the future."

The Federal forces reacted to all this with delight and astonishment. General William Tecumseh Sherman, for one, detected a golden opportunity in the widening rift between the state of Georgia and the Richmond government. "It would be a magnificent stroke of policy," noted the Federal commander, "if we could, without surrendering principle or a foot of ground, arouse the latent enmity of Georgia against Davis."

Sherman invited both Governor Brown and Vice President Stephens to meet with him in Atlanta to discuss terms. His initial offer was to confine Federal troops to the roads and to pay cash for all requisitioned stores if Georgia would pull out of the War.

Confronted with a concrete proposal, both Stephens and Brown backed off from talks, Stephens sputtering that neither Sherman nor he was a duly designated emissary, and Brown observing equivocally that, while Georgia had every legal right to negotiate, honor might not be served by doing so at the particular moment.

Thus the threat of state secession receded for the moment. But the crisis had dispelled

Federal troops in Sherman's army destroy a section of the Macon & Western Central Railroad at Jonesboro, Georgia, by heating the rails red-hot on beds of burning ties, then bending the iron out of shape between two stakes. Sometimes trees were used instead of stakes; the Federals jokingly referred to rails left wrapped around the trunks as "Sherman neckties."

once and for all the tattered illusion of a unified Confederate cause. Citizens, both North and South, had witnessed the near secession of a Confederate state in the midst of war. To the North, this episode provided irrefutable evidence that the enemies of union might be on the brink of warfare among themselves. "While other states and other governors were *arming against the Yankees,*" crowed the New York *World* late in 1864, "Governor Brown was arming *against the confederacy.*" Brown had no such intention, but clearly he and a lot of other Southerners were ready to quit the War.

For Jefferson Davis there was only one issue: independence for the Confederacy. Even through the disastrous autumn of 1864, as Sherman's men rampaged through Georgia toward the sea, the Confederate President insisted that the battered old dream remained attainable. His hopes rested only in part upon a turn of fortune on the battlefield. Just as crucial to the Confederate cause was the possibility of Abraham Lincoln's defeat in the forthcoming U.S. presidential election. The Democratic Party, determined to put an end to the carnage, had laid down what seemed to be an unequivocal peace platform at its convention in Chicago. "After four years of failure to restore the Union by the experiment of war," ran the principal plank, "the public welfare demands that immediate efforts be made for a cessation of hostilities at the earliest practicable moment."

Alexander Stephens welcomed the Democratic platform as "the first ray of light I have seen from the North since the war began." At first Davis, too, showed flashes of optimism that the Northern elections might end the War with Southern honor and independence intact. "The aspect of the peace party was quite encouraging," he wrote, "and the real issue to be decided in the Presidential election was the continuance or cessation of the war."

Even the Republican Party appeared ready to compromise at this juncture. Republican National Chairman Henry Jarvis Raymond asked Lincoln, "Why would it not be wise to appoint a commission to make distinct proffers of peace to Davis on the sole condition of acknowledging the supremacy of the Constitution?" Lincoln, however, was certain that Davis would never be willing to accept such an overture, and he did not bother with it.

The candidate put forward by the Democrats to challenge Lincoln was George B. McClellan, former commanding general of the U.S. Army. Long since dismissed by the President for ineffectiveness in the field, McClellan now yearned for vindication at the polls — ironically cloaked in what seemed the white robe of peace. Rumors of McClellan's pacific tendencies ran rampant through the South. Richmond diarist John Beauchamp Jones recorded a conversation with a woman who had just returned from a stay in the North: "She declares that Gen. McClellan will be elected, and that he is decidedly for peace. She says the peace party would take up arms to put an end to Lincoln's sanguinary career." Davis' friend S. J. Anderson informed him that McClellan would "submit proposals to you which it would be difficult to reject."

Davis was skeptical. Doubting that McClellan's terms for peace would prove palatable, he returned in his speeches to a strident militarism. "Let fresh victories crown our arms," he urged, "and the peace party, if there be such at the North, can elect its candidate."

Davis' doubts were borne out when McClellan announced, "The Union is the one condition of peace — we ask no more." That was like asking Davis for no more than his heart. From that moment, disillusioned Southerners gave up on the notion that McClellan's election might save the Confederacy. In any case, the chances for a Democratic victory now appeared slight. Diarist Jones conceded that "the Peace Party in the United States is not so strong as we supposed."

He was correct. Lincoln was reelected by a wide majority and soon after made it crystal clear to all that the South would receive no favorable terms. "It seems to me," Lincoln said on December 6 in a message to the U.S. Congress, "that no attempt at negotiation with the insurgent leader could result in any good. He would accept nothing short of severance of the Union, precisely what we will not and cannot give. It is an issue which can only be tried by war, and decided by victory."

Lincoln then added, "They can, at any moment, have peace simply by laying down their arms, and submitting to the national authority." He went on to reiterate a prior assurance of "general pardon and amnesty." And lest there be any presumptions or misunderstandings, Lincoln concluded, "I shall not attempt to retract or modify the Emancipation Proclamation, nor shall I return to slavery any person who is free."

The implacable Davis remained determined to fight it out. But now he had virtually nothing to fight with. Only days after Lincoln's address, General Hood lost most

A Stubborn Bishop's Persistent Protest

One of the most faithful practitioners of civil disobedience to Federal rule was William Elder, bishop of St. Mary's Cathedral in Natchez, Mississippi.

When Federal troops occupied the town in July 1863, Elder refused to swear allegiance to the Union. And for an entire year, he withstood demands from Federal officers to include in his services a prayer for the President of the United States. One of the Federals, General Mason Brayman, remained adamant. In July 1864 he warned the bishop, "If you are a patriotic and loyal man, you will read the prayer with pleasure."

Elder again declined, noting in his diary that "the consequences of refusing were in God's own hands." Brayman then exiled Elder to Vidalia, Louisiana.

Two weeks later, General Lorenzo Thomas, who was senior to Brayman, heard of the clergyman's plight. He ordered that Elder be returned to Natchez, and absolved the headstrong bishop once and for all from delivering the presidential prayer.

of the Army of Tennessee in a brief, impetuous campaign around Nashville against impossible odds; his survivors took to the roads. Mary Chesnut, on hearing of the defeat, wrote, "The deep waters are closing over us." Within a matter of days, Sherman received the surrender of Savannah, telegraphing Lincoln that the city's fall was "a Christmas present with 150 heavy guns and plenty of ammunition and also about 25,000 bales of cotton."

Richmond had become a city of desolation under siege. As the bone-chilling rains of late autumn gave way to intermittent snow, one resident wrote, "We can hear distinctly the whistle of shot and shell, and the detonations shake the windows." For the area's bone-weary defenders, many of whom had been on the line for months without leave, there remained only 15 days' rations of bread, most of the meat having been hoarded by speculators. Squads of pressman, called "dogcatchers," roamed Richmond's streets afoot and on horse, arresting any able-bodied men who lacked a pass and dragging them to jail. Those who could certify their exempt status were freed; those who could not were shipped off to the trenches.

By January of 1865, firewood, when it could be found, sold at about $150 a cord. Flour cost more than $425 a barrel — roughly one third more than a well-paid government clerk's monthly wage. The Confederate Congress would huddle in secret session, achieving little, then emerge with disaffected members spouting public denunciations of President Davis. Tennessee Representative Henry Foote was determined to make a separate peace with the Union and struck out for Washington. He was apprehended, however, and brought back to Richmond to face Congressional censure for fleeing to the enemy. Meanwhile, former Secretary of War George Washington Randolph, claiming ill health, boarded a ship for Europe with his family.

Military desertions had become epidemic. Absentees now outnumbered those present for duty. From October 1, 1864, into the early winter of 1865, more than 70,000 Confederate soldiers deserted; officers in a few of Lee's line regiments were said to offer 60 days' furlough to any soldier who shot a deserter. A letter home from the trenches before Richmond in January expressed the general sense of futility: "All of us think we are whipped now. The men, a great portion of them, are ragged and are getting half rashions. Some say we will have to go to Georgey, but the men will not go there."

A litany of military reports confirmed how universal the impulse to desert had become:

"Fifty-six deserted Hill's corps in three days."

"All except forty men deserted the Second Arkansas."

"Eighty-seven abandoned a Tennessee regiment."

One band of soldiers that looted a tannery before departing the battle area in Virginia left a defiant note: "Don't think it was niggers that robbed you. It was 25 North Carolina deserters, and we are going home. We are well armed and hell can't take us."

The weight of accumulating misfortunes began to break Jefferson Davis' health. The President's nerves had been wound too tight for any man to bear. His right arm intermittently became weak and unresponsive, apparently from neuralgia. And as he trudged that winter through the mud and

ELECT LINCOLN

AND THE

BLACK REPUBLICAN TICKET

You will bring on NEGRO EQUALITY, more DEBT, HARDER TIMES, another

DRAFT!

Universal Anarchy, and Ultimate

RUIN!

ELECT McCLELLAN

AND THE WHOLE

Democratic Ticket

You will defeat NEGRO EQUALITY, restore Prosperity, re-establish the

UNION!

In an Honorable, Permanent and Happy

PEACE

An anti-Lincoln poster printed for the U.S. presidential election of 1864 predicts disaster unless voters elect the Democratic candidate, George B. McClellan, former Commander in Chief of the Federal Army. Even though McClellan disavowed such inflammatory rhetoric, Southerners seized on it and prayed for a Democratic victory.

slush of Richmond from house to Executive offices to Congress, hearing as he went the thunder of Grant's guns, he wore a woolen cap that he pulled down over the paralyzed part of his face.

As Davis weakened, his opponents in Congress grew more determined than ever to topple him. Speaker of the House Thomas S. Bocock demanded a purge of Davis' Cabinet. Worse, a circle of Virginia Representa-

tives arrogantly insisted that General Joseph Johnston be restored to a high command post. Secretary of War Seddon, refusing to reinstate Johnston, resigned under the assault, and declined Davis' urgent personal pleas to stay in the government. The Congressional attacks continued. On an astonishing impulse, a group of Congressmen delegated Foreign Affairs Chairman William C. Rives to approach Robert E. Lee and offer the general the dictatorship of the Confederacy, along with a mandate to impose martial law and thus "guide the country through its present crisis."

Horrified at the idea and the obvious conspiracy behind it, Lee refused, asserting that "if the President could not save the country, no one could." Even so, the exhausted Davis finally yielded some of his power, conceding that the consensus "in regard to General R. E. Lee has my full concurrence." And during the third week in January, Congress passed a law that unseated Davis as chief of the Confederate armed forces. A new rank of commander in chief was created — and tendered, of course, to Robert E. Lee. This time the general accepted, though with no particular pleasure or optimism. He assured Davis privately that he did so only to relieve him "from a portion of the constant labor and anxiety which presses upon you." In a quick gesture of appeasement to the anti-Davis crowd, Lee gave Johnston command of the Army of Tennessee.

At long last, Davis also yielded to demands for serious efforts at making peace. While dealing as best he could with the Congressional insurgency, Davis had received an informal envoy from the North, a politician named Francis P. Blair, whom Lincoln had permitted to approach the Confederate President on the understanding that all conversations were to be unofficial. Blair's initial overtures happened to include a wild proposition that he thought might pave the way for a reconciliation of the Union and the Confederacy. He suggested a joint expedition by Confederate and Federal troops against the French puppet, Maximilian, who had seized power in Mexico in clear defiance of the Monroe Doctrine. Blair's bizarre sug-

gestion was ignored by his Southern contacts, but it did serve to open the door to further conversations.

Davis dispatched Blair back to Lincoln with a message: "I am ready to send a commission if you could promise that a commission, minister, or other agent would be received and renew the effort to enter into a conference with a view to secure peace to the two countries. Yours, etc. — Jefferson Davis."

Lincoln shot off a return note, also through Blair: "I have constantly been, am now, and shall continue ready to receive any agent whom he, or any other influential person now resisting the national authority, may informally send me, with a view of securing peace to the people of our common country. Yours, etc. — A. Lincoln." The Union's President thereupon appointed Secretary of State William Seward as the principal spokesman for the United States at any forthcoming conference.

In a clever bit of political manipulation, Davis chose Vice President Stephens, his principal critic and an outspoken peace advocate, to head a three-man Confederate commission that included two other Davis foes, the vociferous Senator R.M.T. Hunter and Judge John A. Campbell. If the three succeeded in their mission, Davis would get the credit for appointing them. If they failed, they would bear the onus. "You are to proceed," Davis wrote in his instructions of January 28, 1865, "for an informal conference upon the issues involved in the existing war, and for the purpose of securing peace to the two countries."

At first, prospects for a negotiated settlement appeared promising. The delegates for both sides set out for Fort Monroe in

In a Southern newspaper cartoon decrying extortionate prices, a poultry vendor extols her gargantuan chickens — bred to stretch like the Confederate dollar — to the miserly owner of a boarding house: "You'll find they go very far. Two cuts in the neck, two on the back, two leg joints, besides the heads."

Hampton Roads, Virginia, where the steamship *River Queen* would serve for a meeting hall. As the three Confederate commissioners passed through the battle lines, the soldiers on both sides cheered them. When they paused at General Grant's headquarters, Grant seemed impressed by their forthrightness — so impressed that he was moved to send a pointed telegram to Washington: "I am convinced that their intentions are good and their desire sincere to restore peace and Union." Then Grant added a veiled suasion for the President: "I am sorry, however, that Mr. Lincoln cannot have an interview with all three."

Lincoln did not ignore the strong signal from his most respected general. Soon a coded cable from Washington reached Seward at Fort Monroe: "Induced by a dispatch from General Grant, I join you as soon as I can come. (Sent in cipher at 9 a.m.) — A. Lincoln."

Next day, February 3, the five men met, Lincoln having made the journey speedily by train to Annapolis, then by steamer to Fort Monroe. As the diminutive Alexander Stephens systematically took off an enormous overcoat and a bundle of woolly shawls in which he had wrapped himself against the cold, Lincoln observed drolly that he had never witnessed "so small a nubbin come out of so much shucks."

For his part, the Confederate Vice President, after a good-natured handshake with Lincoln, went right to business. "Is there no way," he asked, "of putting an end to the present trouble?"

"There was but one way," Lincoln noted later: "for those who were resisting the laws of the Union to cease that resistance. The restoration of the Union is a *sine qua non* with me."

Yet the two sides talked on for more than four hours. At one moment Lincoln offered a ray of hope to the Southern delegates by referring to the Emancipation Proclamation as "a war measure" that would "have effect only from its being an exercise of the war power." And concerning the Constitutional amendment to abolish slavery permanently, now before the U.S. Congress, Seward dropped a tempting hint: "If the Confederate States would abandon the war, they could themselves defeat this amendment.

Varina Howell Davis (*above*),
devoted wife of President Jefferson
Davis, stayed in Richmond with her
husband and four children (*left*) until
the last days of the Confederacy. The
couple lost their first child in infancy;
another boy, four-year-old Joseph,
died in a fall from the Executive
Mansion balcony in April 1864.

The whole number of states being thirty-six, any ten of them could defeat it." Seward went so far as to say, with no demurrer from Lincoln, that if the Confederacy made peace and agreed to abolition, then the United States would be willing to reimburse slaveowners for the loss of their human property.

Had the ultimate issue been slavery, the conflict might have ended then and there. But neither party would budge from its fundamental position: One side held out for independence, the other insisted on restoring the Union.

Lincoln's account of the meeting was curt and to the point: "On the morning of the 3rd," he wrote, "the gentlemen, Messrs. Stephens, Hunter, and Campbell, came aboard of our steamer and had an interview with the Secretary of State and myself. It was not said that in any event or on any condition they ever would consent to reunion." And thus, concluded Abraham Lincoln, "the conference ended without result."

Davis professed great chagrin at the failure of the conference. And he proceeded to put the worst possible face on the conduct of Lincoln and Seward at the meeting—an attempt made easier by the fact that no minutes had been taken and no one was present except the five negotiators. "The Commissioners have returned," Davis announced on February 6. "They were informed that nothing less would be accepted than unconditional submission coupled with the acceptance of recent legislation on the subject of relations between the white and black populations of each state."

Stephens, offended by Davis' misrepresentation of the Northern delegates' remarks on the matter of slavery, refused to cooperate with Davis in distorting Lincoln and Seward's part in the dialogue. When Davis asked Stephens to speak at a Richmond rally, using the alleged outrage at Hampton Roads to stir up the people for a renewed fight, Stephens declined. The Confederate Vice President was so dispirited by the failure of the conference and the all-too-apparent crumbling of the Confederacy that he seemed prepared simply to await the inevitable. "I could not undertake to impress on the minds of the people," he explained later, "the idea that they could do what I believed to be impossible."

He also made it clear to Davis that, for Alexander Stephens, this was the end. Sadly but bluntly, he told the President in Richmond that he would now "go home and stay home." After a moment's silence he added, "And say nothing." A bystander recalled that Stephens then turned and departed, "looking like a walking dead man." He left the capital for the seclusion of his Georgia estate, Liberty Hall, where he remained until he was arrested by Federal troops in the late spring of 1865.

Davis, meanwhile, went ahead with the Richmond rally on his own. Momentarily, he transcended his failing health to hurl, once more, his defiance at the enemy. "What shall we say of the disgrace beneath which we should be buried," Davis asked of the mesmerized crowd, "if we surrender with an army in the field more numerous than that with which Napoleon achieved the glory of France, an army standing among its homesteads?"

Indeed, the Army of Virginia was still in the field, somehow fighting off a force of 125,000 Federals. But now even Robert E. Lee, though loyal and willing to struggle to

---

the end, began to try to make Davis understand that the Confederate troops could not hold out much longer. Patiently he explained to his President that the army "had no subsistence for man or horse, and it could not be gathered in the country. The men, deprived of food and sleep for many days, were worn out and exhausted."

Though he realized it would be futile, Lee attempted to bring a few more men to arms by offering general amnesty to any deserter who would return to his unit within 20 days. Then the general astounded most of his countrymen by endorsing the most desperate policy that any Southerner could conceive: arming the slaves to fight the Federals. "We must decide," said Lee in late February, "whether the negroes shall fight for us, or against us." As a reward for serving the Confederacy, the black soldier should be granted freedom, Lee suggested, and he urged that the government move quickly in the matter, lest "action be deferred until it is too late."

Lee's proposal was greeted with furious protests. R.M.T. Hunter condemned it as the "most pernicious idea that had been suggested since the war began." General Johnston had already branded the arming of slaves a "monstrous proposition." And though Sherman's army was now at the gates of Charleston, that city's *Mercury* insisted: "We want no Confederate Government without our institutions."

But other Southerners viewed Lee's proposal in a more realistic light. Clearly not another Southern white man was ready or willing to fight. And blacks already had proven themselves as front-line troops in Federal units—though with somewhat different motivation.

The Richmond *Examiner*, previously a fierce opponent of such radical ideas, warmed to the prospect of an infusion of fighting men. "General Lee urgently calls for a large force of Negroes," the paper editorialized. "The country will not deny to General Lee *anything* he may ask for." Secretary of State Judah Benjamin concurred, "Let us say to every negro who wishes to go into the ranks, 'Go and fight—you are free.'" Caught up in the tide, President Davis admitted that the need for black soldiers "is now becoming daily more evident." General Longstreet, fighting to hold off the enemy on the north bank of the James River, even requested that a "company of negroes be sent down to his lines" to demonstrate their effectiveness.

Responding to such pressure, the Confederate Congress on the 13th of March passed a bill that called for the mustering of 300,000 black soldiers. And at 4:30 on the afternoon

A sketch from a Northern newspaper shows two fully armed blacks serving as pickets in the Confederate Army as a Federal officer purportedly saw them through his field glass at Fredericksburg, Virginia, in January 1863. In fact, no blacks ever served as fighting troops in the Confederate Army, although in the desperate final months of the War, the Congress in Richmond authorized using them.

of Sunday, March 19, the citizens of Richmond were treated to a display that they had scarcely dreamed possible. A battalion of three white companies — convalescents at the city's Chimborazo Hospital — and two black companies, orderlies at the same hospital, marched together down Main Street toward Capitol Square, led by a brass band playing "Dixie."

The men were without uniforms, but at least they had weapons and appropriate music. On reaching the square, the novel battalion wheeled right to face the Capitol, whose windows were filled with spectators, and proceeded to perform the manual of arms. So impressive were they that, next day, the Richmond *Whig* reported with satisfaction that "Sambo could be taught to handle a gun as well as the hoe."

But no blacks would ever fight for the Confederacy. On April 2, 1865, just two weeks after the parade, Richmond's defenses collapsed. The War was all but over. Braxton Bragg, with only 6,500 men, had evacuated Wilmington, North Carolina, leaving the Confederacy without an Atlantic seaport. Johnston, who had held off Sherman's masses in late March, was bled white by that final, futile bit of gallantry. Jubal Early's tattered force in the Shenandoah Valley had been decimated by Philip Sheridan. The fields, forests and small towns of the dissolving Confederacy were crawling with stragglers trying to get home.

In the capital Jefferson Davis packed his family onto one of the last, creaking trains as it prepared to leave the city. Admonishing his wife that he was not sure he would ever see her again, he pressed upon her a small pistol and showed her how to use it. Then he started back into his city, appearing, in the words of a close friend, "old, grey and wrinkled."

Desperate citizens were trying to push themselves and a few cherished belongings onto other trains already overladen with government officials, reams of secret archives, and the last of the Confederate government's specie. In town, others were simply attempting to hide what valuables they possessed — furniture, cattle, silver plate, clothing — in cellars, attics or yards to keep it away from looters. A few traders, wildly optimistic, were even trying to sell or buy slaves for five or ten dollars in gold. Then the destruction began.

At dawn on April 3 terrifying explosions shook the city — first the blasting by Confederates of their last warships on the James River, then the detonation of the city's powder magazine. Fires that had started during the night when Lee's men torched cotton, tobacco and food warehouses to deprive the advancing Federals became a billowing inferno. When the flames reached the city's armory, it erupted with thousands of bursting shells, throwing howling fragments across the city and coating sidewalks with shards of glass. All morning a cacophony of explosions reverberated through Richmond. The flames leaped and crackled along Main Street, consuming a swath of buildings in the business and residential districts.

In late morning the Federal troops arrived. Among them were black soldiers, who were joyously cheered by Richmond's black residents, now indisputably free. As the men of the Union streamed into the city from the east, the last of the Confederate troops surged out southward across the James, taking with them what food they could find and throwing open stores and

warehouses to the people. Confederate bonds and paper money littered the streets. Acrid smoke from fires and explosions seeped into every corner of the capital.

Richmond officials, in an effort to prevent drunken mayhem, broke open whiskey and rum kegs and emptied the contents into the gutters. "The rougher elements of the population, white and black alike, were dipping up the vile stuff with their hands," an eyewitness reported, "and pouring it down their throats. The shrill whistle of locomotives sounded loud and frequent in the near distance, as train after train hurried away bearing frantic citizens. Bands of thieves and rascals of every degree, broken loose from the penitentiary, were entering the stores on either side of the street and stealing whatever they could lay their hands upon, while the entire black population seemed out of doors and crazy with delight. Tumult, violence, riot, pillage, everywhere prevailed, and as if these were not enough to illustrate the horrors of war, the roar of the flames, the clanging of bells, and general uproar and confusion were sufficient to appall the stoutest heart."

Undamaged, high above the turmoil, stood the sharp profile of the Confederate Capitol, designed by Thomas Jefferson. In this building Lee had received command of the Virginia troops, Stonewall Jackson's body had lain in state, and legislators had defiantly sworn that the Confederate States of America would stand forever. Now, as hundreds of refugees huddled in its shadows, seeking shelter from the showers of cinders, from the rooftop flew two red, white and blue Federal cavalry guidons and a huge American flag.

ACKNOWLEDGMENTS

The editors thank the following individuals and institutions for their help in the preparation of this volume:
Alabama: Birmingham — Betty Keen, Birmingham Museum of Art. Montgomery — Robert Cason, Alabama Department of Archives and History. Tuscaloosa — Clark Center, Deborah Nygren, William Stanley Hoole Special Collections, University of Alabama Library.
California: San Marino — Brita Mack, Virginia Renner, Huntington Library.
Connecticut: Hartford — Roberta Bradford, Stowe-Day Foundation.
Delaware: Greenville — John Williams, Eleutherian Mills Historical Library.
Georgia: Athens — Mary Ellen Brooks, Vesta Lee Gordon, Robert M. Willingham Jr., Special Collections, University of Georgia Libraries; Charles East. Augusta — Virginia E. de Treville, Augusta Richmond County Museum. Savannah — Barbara Bennett, Georgia Historical Society; Mrs. Gerald Fling and the United Daughters of the Confederacy. Washington — Rita Gravenor, Doris Martin, Washington Wilkes Historical Museum.
Illinois: Chicago — Olivia Mahoney, Maureen O'Brien Will, Chicago Historical Society. Springfield — Mary Michals, Illinois State Historical Society.
Indiana: Bloomington — Saundra Taylor, Manuscripts Department, Lilly Library, Indiana University. Rensselaer — Catherine A. Salyers, Ethel Yoder, Jasper County Public Library.
Louisiana: Baton Rouge — M. Stone Miller, Don Morrison, Department of Archives and Manuscripts, Troy H. Middleton Library, Louisiana State University. New Orleans — Pat Eymard, Confederate Memorial Hall; Wilbur E. Meneray, Howard-Tilton Memorial Library, Tulane University.
Maryland: Towson — Peter Bardaglio.
Massachusetts: Boston — Ellie Reichlin, Society for the Preservation of New England Antiquities.
Michigan: Ann Arbor — Barbara Mitchell, William L. Clements Library, University of Michigan.
Mississippi: Natchez — Joan W. Gandy, Myrtle Bank Galleries; Vicksburg — Gordon A. Cotton, Old Court House Museum, Eva Davis Memorial.
New Jersey: Basking Ridge — Mrs. Hendrik B. von Rensselaer.
New York: Greenport — Frederick S. Lightfoot, Lightfoot Collection.
North Carolina: Chapel Hill — Richard A. Shrader, Wilson Library, University of North Carolina. Durham — Timothy D. Pyatt, William R. Perkins Library, Duke University. Greensboro — Susan Webster, Greensboro Historical Museum. Wilmington — Susan Applegate Krouse, New Hanover County Museum.
Ohio: Cleveland — Charles Sherrill, Western Reserve Historical Society.
Pennsylvania: Carlisle — Michael S. Winey, U.S. Army Military History Institute. Wayne — Russ Pritchard.
Rhode Island: Providence — Jennifer Lee, John Hay Library, Brown University.
South Carolina: Columbia — LaVerne Watson, South Carolina Confederate Relic Room and Museum.
Vermont: Montpelier — Mary Pat Brigham, Vermont Historical Society.
Virginia: Alexandria — Frank and Marie-T. Wood. Ashland — Dr. and Mrs. Bruce English. Falls Church — Charles Nelson. Richmond — Cathy Carlson, David Hahn, Museum of the Confederacy; Edie Jeter, Sarah Shields, Valentine Museum; Rosemary Arneson, Patricia Taylor, Virginia State Library. Stratford — Ralph Draughon, Jessie Ball duPont Memorial Library, Stratford Hall.
Washington, D.C.: Eveline Nave, Information Unit, Library of Congress; L. W. Vosloh, National Numismatic Collections, National Museum of American History, Smithsonian Institution; Suzanne Embree, Monroe Fabian, National Portrait Gallery, Smithsonian Institution; James Harrison, and Elizabeth Zibrat, Otis Historical Archives, Walter Reed Army Medical Center; Agnes Hoover, David Koronberger, Naval Historical Center, Washington Navy Yard.

The index for this book was prepared by Nicholas J. Anthony.

PICTURE CREDITS

Credits from left to right are separated by semicolons, from top to bottom by dashes.

Cover: Painting by Gilbert Gaul, from the collection of the Birmingham Museum of Art, gift of John E. Meyer, photographed by George Flemming. 2, 3: Map by Peter McGinn. 9-16: Library of Congress. 18: Painting by D. J. Kennedy, courtesy The Franklin D. Roosevelt Library — Washington Wilkes Historical Museum, photographed by Michael W. Thomas. 19: Courtesy Russ A. Pritchard, photographed by Larry Sherer; courtesy New Hanover County Museum, photographed by William J. Boney Jr. — Greensboro Historical Museum, Greensboro, North Carolina, photographed by L. Atkinson — courtesy New Hanover County Museum, photographed by William J. Boney Jr. — Confederate Memorial Hall, New Orleans, Louisiana, photographed by Bill van Calsem; Special Collection of the Armed Forces Medical Museum, Washington, D.C., photographed by Steve Tuttle. 20: Library of Congress. 21: Library of Congress, inset, courtesy of Augusta Richmond County Museum. 22: Confederate Imprints Collection, the University of Georgia Libraries. 24, 25: Library of Congress. 26: Museum of the Confederacy, Richmond, Virginia, photographed by Larry Sherer. 27: Library of Congress. 28: Courtesy Frank & Marie-T. Wood Print Collections, Alexandria, Virginia. 30: Painting by Samuel Osgood, National Portrait Gallery, Smithsonian Institution, Washington, D.C., on loan from Serena Williams Miles Van Rensselaer. 31: Kean Archives, Philadelphia. 32, 33: From *Le Monde illustré*, courtesy Musée de la Marine, Paris. 34, 35: Courtesy Frank & Marie-T. Wood Print Collections, Alexandria, Virginia. 36, 37: Courtesy Frank & Marie-T. Wood Print Collections, Alexandria, Virginia; from *Battles and Leaders of the Civil War*, Grant-Lee Edition, Vol. II, The Century Co., New York, © 1884. 38, 39: Courtesy Frank & Marie-T. Wood Print Collections, Alexandria, Virginia; from *Prison-Life in the Tobacco Warehouse at Richmond*, by Lieut. Wm. C. Harris, published by George W. Childs, Philadelphia, Pa., 1862. 40, 41: Courtesy Frank & Marie-T. Wood Print Collections, Alexandria, Virginia. 43: Lithograph by J. B. Guibet, courtesy Confederate Memorial Hall, New Orleans, Louisiana, photographed by Bill van Calsem. 44, 45: Library of Congress. 47: United Daughters of the Confederacy, from collection on deposit at the Georgia Historical Society, Savannah, Georgia, photographed by Daniel Grantham — Chicago Historical Society, photographed by Robert Frerck; Alabama Department of Archives and History, photographed by John Scott(2). 49: Maryland Historical Society, Baltimore. 50: U.S. Army Military History Institute, copied by Robert Walch. 51: Jessie Ball duPont Memorial Library, Stratford Hall, photographed by Larry Sherer. 52: Confederate Imprints Collection, the University of Georgia Libraries. 53, 54: Library of Congress. 55: Confederate Imprints Collection, the University of Georgia Libraries, photographed by Michael W. Thomas. 56, 57: Library of Congress. 58: From the Rare Book Department of Perkins Library, Duke University. 59: Valentine Museum, Richmond, Virginia. 60: Painting by William L. Sheppard, Museum of the Confederacy, Richmond, Virginia. 62, 63: Courtesy Russ A. Pritchard, photographed by Larry Sherer. 64, 65: Courtesy Russ A. Pritchard, photographed by Larry Sherer(2) — Museum of the Confederacy, Richmond, Virginia, photographed by Larry Sherer; courtesy Russ A. Pritchard, photographed by Larry Sherer(3) — Museum of the Confederacy, Richmond, Virginia, photographed by Larry Sherer; courtesy Russ A. Pritchard, photographed by Larry Sherer. 66: Museum of the Confederacy, Richmond, Virginia, photographed by Larry Sherer — South Carolina Confederate Relic Room and Museum, Columbia, South Carolina. 67: Museum of the Confederacy, Richmond, Virginia, photographed by Larry Sherer. 68, 69: National Numismatic Collections, National Museum of American History, Smithsonian Institution, Washington, D.C., photographed by Henry Beville. 70-73: Courtesy Chris Nelson. 76: Courtesy Frank & Marie-T. Wood Print Collections, Alexandria, Virginia. 78: Library of Congress. 79: Department of Cultural Resources, North Carolina Division of Archives and History, Raleigh, North Carolina. 81: Library of Congress — National Archives Neg. No. 200(S)-M-32. 83: W. S. Hoole Special Collection, The University of Alabama Library. 85: Courtesy Frank & Marie-T. Wood Print Collections, Alexandria, Virginia. 87: Library of Congress. 88: Courtesy Frank & Marie-T. Wood Print Collections, Alexandria, Virginia. 90: Library of Congress. 92: From *The Book Anecdotes and Incidents of the War of the Rebellion*, by Frazar Kirkland, Hartford Publishing Co., Hartford, Conn., 1866. 94: Courtesy Frank & Marie-T. Wood Print Collections, Alexandria, Virginia. 96, 97: From *A Confederate Girl's Diary*, by Sarah Morgan Dawson, published by Houghton Mifflin Company, Boston and New York, 1913; Albert Shaw Collection, Review of Reviews *Photographic History of the Civil War*, copied by Larry Sherer. 98, 99: U.S. Army Military History Institute, copied by Robert Walch, inset, Department of Archives and Manuscripts, Louisiana State University, Baton Rouge, Louisiana. 100-105: Department of Archives and Manuscripts, Louisiana State University, Baton Rouge, Louisiana. 106, 107: Department of Archives and Manuscripts, Louisiana State University, Baton Rouge, Louisiana, except left, U.S. Army Military History Institute, copied by Robert Walch. 108, 109: Department of Archives and Manuscripts, Louisiana State University, Baton Rouge, Louisiana; Illinois State Historical Museum, Richmond, Virginia. 112, 113: Courtesy Frank & Marie-T. Wood Print Collections, Alexandria, Virginia. 114: Manuscripts Department, Tulane University Library — Rosemonde E. and Emile Kuntz Collection, Manuscripts Department, Tulane University Library. 115: Courtesy Frank & Marie-T. Wood Print Collections, Alexandria, Virginia. 116: Library of Congress. 117: Courtesy Frank & Marie-T. Wood Print Collections, Alexandria, Virginia. 118, 119: Library of Congress, inset

Manuscripts Department, Lilly Library, Indiana University, Bloomington, Indiana. 120: Courtesy the Society for the Preservation of New England Antiquities, Boston. 122: The Lightfoot Collection. 124, 125: Painting by Xanthus P. Smith, courtesy Kennedy Galleries, Inc., New York. 127: Hagley Museum and Library, Greenville, Delaware — Naval Historical Center, Navy Department, donation of E. D. Sloan Jr., Greenville, South Carolina. 129: Courtesy Frank & Marie-T. Wood Print Collections, Alexandria, Virginia. 130, 131: Courtesy Vermont Historical Society. 132: Library of Congress. 133: McLellan Lincoln Collection, John Hay Library, Brown University. 134, 135: Library of Congress; U.S. Army Military History Institute, copied by Robert Walch. 136-139: Western Reserve Historical Society. 140, 141: The Lightfoot Collection, inset, printed through the courtesy of the Rensselaer Public Library, Rensselaer, Indiana. 142, 143: The Stowe-Day Foundation, Hartford, Connecticut; U.S. Army Military History Institute, copied by Robert Walch. 144, 145: National Archives Neg. No. 111-B-400; Library of Congress. 146, 147: Library of Congress. 149: Courtesy Frank & Marie-T. Wood Print Collections, Alexandria, Virginia. 150: The Huntington Library, San Marino, California. 152, 153: Maps by William L. Hezlep. 154: Old Court House Museum, Vicksburg. 156, 157: Courtesy Frank & Marie-T. Wood Print Collections, Alexandria, Virginia. 159: Myrtle Bank Galleries, Natchez, Mississippi. 161: Louis A. Warren Lincoln Library and Museum, Fort Wayne, Indiana. 163, 164: Library of Congress. 166: Courtesy Frank & Marie-T. Wood Print Collections, Alexandria, Virginia. 168, 169: Valentine Museum, Richmond, Virginia.

BIBLIOGRAPHY

Books

Andrews, J. Cutler, *The South Reports the Civil War*. Princeton University Press, 1970.

Black, Robert C., III, *The Railroads of the Confederacy*. The University of North Carolina Press, 1952.

Blassingame, John W., ed., *Slave Testimony: Two Centuries of Letters, Speeches, Interviews, and Autobiographies*. Louisiana State University Press, 1977.

Boatner, Mark Mayo, III, *The Civil War Dictionary*. David McKay Company, Inc., 1959.

Botts, John Minor, *The Great Rebellion: Its Secret History, Rise, Progress, and Disastrous Failure*. Harper & Brothers, Publishers, 1866.

Bryan, T. Conn, *Confederate Georgia*. University of Georgia Press, 1953.

Carse, Robert, *Department of the South: Hilton Head Island in the Civil War*. The State Printing Company, 1981.

Chesnut, Mary, *Mary Chesnut's Civil War*. Ed. by C. Vann Woodward. Yale University Press, 1981.

Cohen, Stan, *The Civil War in West Virginia: A Pictorial History*. Pictorial Histories Publishing Company, 1982.

Cole, Arthur C., *The Irrepressible Conflict, 1850-1865 (A History of American Life*, Vol. 7). Quadrangle Books, Inc., 1971.

Commager, Henry Steele, ed., *The Blue and the Gray: The Story of the Civil War as Told by Participants*, Vol. 2. The Bobbs-Merrill Company, 1973.

Coulter, E. Merton, *The Confederate States of America, 1861-1865 (A History of the South*, Vol. 7). Louisiana State University Press, 1950.

Craven, Avery, *The Coming of the Civil War*. The University of Chicago Press, 1957.

Cumming, Kate, *Kate: The Journal of a Confederate Nurse*. Ed. by Richard Barksdale Harwell. Louisiana State University Press, 1959.

Curry, Richard Orr, *A House Divided: A Study of Statehood Politics and the Copperhead Movement in West Virginia*. University of Pittsburgh Press, 1964.

Dabney, Virginius, *Richmond: The Story of a City*. Doubleday & Company, Inc., 1976.

Dannett, Sylvia G. L., *A Treasury of Civil War Humor*. Thomas Yoseloff, 1963.

Davis, Jefferson:
Jefferson Davis: Private Letters, 1823-1889. Ed. by Hudson Strode. Harcourt, Brace & World, Inc., 1966.
The Rise and Fall of the Confederate Government, Vols. 1 and 2. D. Appleton and Company, 1881.

Davis, Varina, *Jefferson Davis: Ex-President of the Confederate States of America*, Vol. 2. Belford Company, Publishers, 1890.

Davis, William C., *The Embattled Confederacy (The Image of War, 1861-1865*, Vol. 3). Doubleday & Company, Inc., 1982.

Dawson, Sarah Morgan, *A Confederate Girl's Diary*. Ed. by James I. Robertson Jr. Greenwood Press, Publishers, 1972.

Degler, Carl N., *The Other South: Southern Dissenters in the Nineteenth Century*. Harper & Row, 1974.

Dew, Charles B., *Ironmaker to the Confederacy: Joseph R. Anderson and the Tredegar Iron Works*. Yale University Press, 1966.

Dinkins, James, *1861-1865, by an Old Johnnie: Personal Recollections and Experiences in the Confederate Army*. Press of Morningside Bookshop, 1975.

Dowdey, Clifford, *Experiment in Rebellion*. Doubleday & Company, Inc., 1946.

East, Charles, *Baton Rouge: A Civil War Album*. Charles East, 1977.

Eaton, Clement:
A History of the Old South: The Emergence of a Reluctant Nation. Macmillan Publishing Co., Inc., 1975.
A History of the Southern Confederacy. The Macmillan Company, 1954.
Jefferson Davis. The Free Press, 1977.
The Waning of the Old South Civilization, 1860-1880's. University of Georgia Press, 1968.

Edwards, William B., *Civil War Guns*. Castle Books, 1962.

Escott, Paul D., *After Secession: Jefferson Davis and the Failure of Confederate Nationalism*. Louisiana State University Press, 1978.

Fleming, Walter L., *Civil War and Reconstruction in Alabama*. The Reprint Company, Publishers, 1978.

Freeman, Douglas Southall:
Lee's Lieutenants: A Study in Command, Vol. 1. Charles Scribner's Sons, 1942.
R. E. Lee: A Biography, Vol. 1. Charles Scribner's Sons, 1934.

Fuller, Claud E., and Richard D. Steuart, *Firearms of the Confederacy*. Quarterman Publications, Inc., 1944.

Gerteis, Louis S., *From Contraband to Freedman: Federal Policy toward Southern Blacks, 1861-1865*. Greenwood Press, Inc., 1973.

Goff, Richard D., *Confederate Supply*. Duke University Press, 1969.

Guernsey, Alfred H., and Henry M. Alden, *Harper's Pictorial History of the Civil War*. The Fairfax Press, 1866.

Harwell, Richard B., *Confederate Music*. The University of North Carolina Press, 1950.

Henry, Robert Selph, *The Story of the Confederacy*. Peter Smith, 1970.

Jones, J. B., *A Rebel War Clerk's Diary at the Confederate States Capital*, Vols. 1 and 2. J. B. Lippincott & Co., 1866.

Jones, Katharine M., ed.:
Heroines of Dixie: Spring of High Hopes. Mockingbird Books, 1974.

Heroines of Dixie: Winter of Desperation. Mockingbird Books, 1974.

Kerby, Robert L., *Kirby Smith's Confederacy: The Trans-Mississippi South, 1863-1865*. Columbia University Press, 1972.

Kimmel, Stanley, *Mr. Davis's Richmond*. Coward-McCann, Inc., 1958.

Kirkland, Frazar, *The Pictorial Book of Anecdotes and Incidents of the War of the Rebellion*. Hartford Publishing Co., 1866.

LeConte, Joseph, *'Ware Sherman: A Journal of Three Months' Personal Experience in the Last Days of the Confederacy*. University of California Press, 1937.

Litwack, Leon F., *Been in the Storm So Long: The Aftermath of Slavery*. Alfred A. Knopf, 1979.

Long, E. B., *The Civil War Day by Day: An Almanac, 1861-1865*. Doubleday & Company, Inc., 1971.

Lonn, Ella, *Desertion during the Civil War*. Peter Smith, 1966.

McCardell, John, *The Idea of a Southern Nation: Southern Nationalists and Southern Nationalism, 1830-1860*. W. W. Norton & Company, 1979.

McDonald, Cornelia, *A Diary with Reminiscences of the War and Refugee Life in the Shenandoah Valley, 1860-1865*. Cullom & Ghertner Co., 1934.

McElroy, Robert, *Jefferson Davis: The Unreal and the Real*, Vols. 1 and 2. Kraus Reprint Co., 1969.

McGuire, Judith W., *Diary of a Southern Refugee during the War*. Arno Press, 1972.

McPherson, James M., *The Negro's Civil War*. Vintage Books, 1965.

Massey, Mary Elizabeth:
Ersatz in the Confederacy. University of South Carolina Press, 1952.
Refugee Life in the Confederacy. Louisiana State University Press, 1964.

Meade, Robert Douthat, *Judah P. Benjamin: Confederate Statesman*. Oxford University Press, 1943.

Merrell, W. H., *Five Months in Rebeldom; or Notes from the Diary of a Bull Run Prisoner, at Richmond*. Adams & Dabney, 1862.

Moore, Albert Burton, *Conscription and Conflict in the Confederacy*. Hillary House Publishers Ltd., 1963.

Moore, Frank, ed., *The Rebellion Record: A Diary of American Events*, Vols. 1-4. D. Van Nostrand, 1867.

Myers, Robert Manson, ed., *The Children of Pride: A True Story of Georgia and the Civil War*. Yale University Press, 1972.

Nevins, Allan, *The Organized War, 1863-1864 (The War for the Union*, Vol. 3). Charles Scribner's Sons, 1971.

Owsley, Frank Lawrence, *King Cotton Diplomacy: Foreign Relations of the Confederate States of America*. The University of Chicago Press, 1959.

Paludan, Phillip Shaw, *Victims: A True Story of the Civil War.* The University of Tennessee Press, 1981.
Patrick, Rembert W., *Jefferson Davis and His Cabinet.* Louisiana State University Press, 1944.
Pember, Phoebe Yates, *A Southern Woman's Story: Life in Confederate Richmond.* Ed. by Bell Irvin Wiley. Mockingbird Books, 1974.
Putnam, Sallie A. B., *Richmond during the War: Four Years of Personal Observation.* G. W. Carleton & Co., Publishers, 1867.
Ramey, Emily G., and John K. Gott, *The Years of Anguish: Fauquier County, Virginia, 1861-1865.* The Fauquier County Civil War Centennial Committee, 1965.
Ringold, May Spencer, *The Role of the State Legislatures in the Confederacy.* University of Georgia Press, 1966.
Roark, James L., *Masters without Slaves: Southern Planters in the Civil War and Reconstruction.* W. W. Norton & Company, 1977.
Roland, Charles P., *The Confederacy.* The University of Chicago Press, 1960.
Schwab, John Christopher, *The Confederate States of America, 1861-1865.* Charles Scribner's Sons, 1901.
Silver, James W., *Confederate Morale and Church Propaganda.* Confederate Publishing Company, Inc., 1957.
Simkins, Francis Butler, and James Welch Patton, *The Women of the Confederacy.* Garrett and Massie, Incorporated, 1936.
Skipper, Ottis Clark, *J.D.B. De Bow: Magazinist of the Old South.* University of Georgia Press, 1958.
Smith, Page, *Trial by Fire: A People's History of the Civil War and Reconstruction.* McGraw-Hill Book Company, 1982.
Strode, Hudson, *Jefferson Davis, Tragic Hero: The Last Twenty-five Years, 1864-1889.* Harcourt, Brace & World,

Inc., 1964.
Tatum, Georgia Lee, *Disloyalty in the Confederacy.* The University of North Carolina Press, 1934.
Thomas, Emory M.:
The Confederacy as a Revolutionary Experience. Prentice-Hall, Inc., 1971.
The Confederate Nation, 1861-1865. Harper & Row, Publishers, 1979.
The Confederate State of Richmond: A Biography of the Capital. University of Texas Press, 1971.
Thornton, J. Mills, III, *Politics and Power in a Slave Society: Alabama, 1800-1860.* Louisiana State University Press, 1978.
Todd, Frederick P., *American Military Equipage, 1851-1872.* Charles Scribner's Sons, 1980.
Todd, Richard Cecil, *Confederate Finance.* The University of Georgia Press, 1954.
Tucker, Glenn, *Zeb Vance: Champion of Personal Freedom.* The Bobbs-Merrill Company, Inc., 1965.
United States War Department, *The War of the Rebellion: A Compilation of the Official Records of the Union and Confederate Armies.* Government Printing Office, 1902.
Vandiver, Frank E.:
Ploughshares into Swords: Josiah Gorgas and Confederate Ordnance. University of Texas Press, 1952.
Their Tattered Flags. Harper & Row, 1970.
Von Abele, Rudolph, *Alexander H. Stephens: A Biography.* Negro Universities Press, 1971.
Warner, Ezra J., and W. Buck Yearns, *Biographical Register of the Confederate Congress.* Louisiana State University Press, 1975.
Wharton, H. M., *War Songs and Poems of the Southern Confederacy, 1861-1865.* H. M. Wharton, 1904.

Wiley, Bell Irvin:
The Life of Johnny Reb: The Common Soldier of the Confederacy. Louisiana State University Press, 1980.
The Plain People of the Confederacy. Peter Smith, 1971.
Southern Negroes, 1861-1865. Louisiana State University Press, 1965.
Wiley, Bell Irvin, and Hirst D. Milhollen, *Embattled Confederates: An Illustrated History of Southerners at War.* Bonanza Books, 1964.
Wilson, Edmund, *Patriotic Gore: Studies in the Literature of the American Civil War.* Oxford University Press, 1962.
Wyatt-Brown, Bertram, *Southern Honor: Ethics and Behavior in the Old South.* Oxford University Press, 1982.
Yearns, Wilfred Buck, *The Confederate Congress.* The University of Georgia Press, 1960.

Other Sources
Daniel, Larry J., "Manufacturing Cannon in the Confederacy." *Civil War Times Illustrated,* November 1973.
De Bow's Review, September 1861.
Holmes, Jack D. L., "The Mississippi County That 'Seceded' from the Confederate States of America." *Civil War Times Illustrated,* February 1965.
Kimball, William J., "The Bread Riot in Richmond, 1863." *Civil War History,* June 1961.
Melton, Maurice, " 'A Grand Assemblage': George W. Rains and the Augusta Powder Works." *Civil War Times Illustrated,* January 1973.
Pettigrew, William, William Pettigrew Family Papers, #592, Southern Historical Collection, The University of North Carolina at Chapel Hill.
Tice, Douglas O., "The Richmond Bread Riot." *Civil War Times Illustrated,* February 1974.

INDEX